Christmas, 1987

Dear Lisa and John,

In our on-going attempt to prove to you that Washington has its own ~ architectural charms, we thought this volume might aid our cause. Hope you enjoy it.

Love,

Jerry and Eileen

P.S. Personally conducted walking tours of these sights are always available ☺

DECO

ART DECO DESIGN IN THE NATION'S CAPITAL

HANS WIRZ AND RICHARD STRINER

SMITHSONIAN INSTITUTION PRESS
WASHINGTON, D.C. 1984

Unless otherwise noted, photographs are by Hans Wirz.

The paper in this book meets the guidelines for permanence
and durability of the Committee
on Production Guidelines for
Book Longevity of the Council on Library Resources.

Library of Congress Cataloging in Publication Data

Wirz, Hans.
　Washington deco.

　Bibliography: p.
　Includes index.
　Supt. of Docs. no.: SI 1.2:D35
　1. Washington (D.C.)—Buildings.　2. Art deco—
Washington (D.C.)　3. Decoration and ornament,
Architectural—Washington (D.C.)　4. Architecture, Modern—
20th century—Washington (D.C.)　I. Striner, Richard,
1950–　.　II. Title.
NA735.W3W57 1984　720'.9753　84-600183
ISBN 0-87474-970-0 (alk. paper)

CONTENTS

Resplendent, even in its semi-industrial setting, the Hecht's warehouse building of 1937 is a jewellike fantasy creation in the medium of glass brick. The building is one of the most significant industrial Deco buildings in the world.

Supple curves of the Deco buildings in Glen Echo Amusement Park encouraged the visitor to "come and play" in the "Cuddle-Up," "Laff In The Dark," and the "Spanish Ballroom."

The bright marquee of the Senator Theater, designed by John J. Zink, was a persuasive invitation to sample the latest Hollywood fare. The theater, still in use on Minnesota Avenue, NE, retains a stunning original streamlined Deco lobby.

Decorative plasterwork enhances the blue monochromatic treatment of the lobby in the Delano Apartments, designed by George T. Santmyers and completed in 1941. When beheld in the evening, the glowing lobby seems to symbolize the siren call of the modern metropolis.

Formica surfaces help to merge elegance with functional merit in the lobby of 1417 N Street, NW. The appearance of natural wood permitted richness of texture and bold geometric design to be successfully combined.

The warm tones of natural wood veneer combine with the sweep of cove lighting, giving the lobby of the 2800 Woodley Road apartment building a suave appeal that was suited to the age of Fred Astaire and Ginger Rogers. The building, designed by George T. Santmyers, was completed in 1941.

Light and shade play over the tile mosaics framing the entrance to the Cafritz apartment building at 1020 19th Street, NW. The 1938 building, the Gwenwood, was named for Gwen Cafritz, the wife of construction magnate Morris Cafritz. The building was demolished in 1981.

Bold ziggurat soars above the roofline of High Towers, a Cafritz apartment on 16th Street, NW. In the 1960s an alternate name was proposed for the zigzag variant of twenties and thirties design: "Aztec Airways."

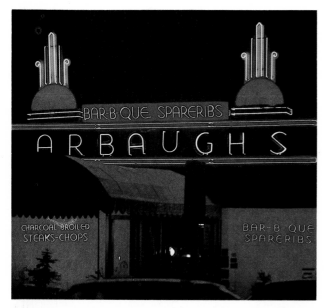

A spirited neon sign advertises Arbaugh's, a Deco sparerib palace that opened on Connecticut Avenue in 1938. Though the restaurant recently closed, much of the original decor will be retained in the building, thanks to the efforts of the Art Deco Society of Washington.

An undoubted masterpiece of John Joseph Earley, this elaborate concrete mosaic ceiling was produced for the Justice Department Building in the Federal Triangle. The ceiling panels, on display in the mid-block gateway entrance to the building on 10th Street, NW, were first hung in place, and only then—for the sake of structural permanence—was the concrete poured for the floor and ceiling above, an ingenious reversal of normal construction techniques.

This close-up view of polychrome concrete mosaic illustrates the texture of John Joseph Earley's favorite building material. The colors have retained their brilliance for fifty years in the harshest weather conditions as a result of the extreme pride of craftsmanship displayed by the Earley studio in Rosslyn, Virginia.

The painstaking sense of detail to be found in Deco-era craftsmanship can be seen in the delicate etched-glass panels of a decorative exterior lamp at the southern entrance to the Library of Congress Annex.

The ubiquitous Deco plant or lotus motif of the Deco era, here displayed in the first-floor elevator lobby of the Library of Congress Annex, was replicated throughout the building. The motif was carved by hand in the marble wainscoting and even stamped on the backs of the wooden reading-room chairs.

Lustrous aluminum and bronze were employed for the decorative elevator doors of the 1939 Library of Congress Annex. The architects, Pierson and Wilson, took care to leave detailed instructions on the future care and cleaning of the building's decorative metalwork.

13

FOREWORD

One of the most overlooked and unappreciated periods in the long architectural history of Washington, D.C., during the past 193 years is that of the Art Deco era, which covered the years 1925–1945. *Washington Deco* by Richard Striner, historian, and Hans Wirz, architect, at last successfully corrects this situation. During the past six years the authors have located and cataloged more than 400 Art Deco buildings in Washington, D.C., and its Maryland and Virginia suburbs. They include a variety of building types, such as banks, theaters, warehouses, churches, apartment houses, stores, restaurants, as well as houses, scattered throughout the metropolitan area.

Washington Deco not only performs an important function in listing and describing the surviving local Art Deco buildings but also in discussing the origin of the style at the Paris exposition of 1925 and the variations of this design movement, including zigzag, streamlined, and Greco-Deco. Washington's Art Deco buildings are different from those of other American cities, not only because they are more restrained in design but also because they usually combine both the zigzag phase associated with the 1920s and the streamlined phase related to the 1930s.

Art Deco was a delightful interlude, a transitional period between Beaux Arts and the International Style. In addition to the New York architects who contributed to Washington's architectural heritage, such as the firm of Abbot, Merkt and Company, which designed the award-winning Hecht Company Warehouse, and Voorhees, Gmelin and Walker, which was responsible for the Chesapeake and Potomac Telephone Company Building, a number of skilled local architects produced significant works. The authors, for example, discuss the numerous Art Deco apartment houses by Alvin Aubinoe and Harry L. Edwards of the Cafritz Company, as well as buildings designed by George T. Santmyers, Joseph Abel, and John J. Zink. The Washington sculptor and innovator, John Joseph Earley, left a national reputation because of his invention and use of the prefab concrete mosaic house construction, of which several Art Deco examples survive in the Maryland suburbs.

In addition to the location of numerous privately owned structures, Messrs. Striner and Wirz have identified a number of federal government buildings with significant Art Deco treatments of either the façades or interior spaces. What a breathtaking experience to view for the first time the dazzling elevator lobbies, law library, and auditorium of the Department of Justice Building, as well as the nine-story-high circular staircases of the Post Office Building—Art Deco masterpieces hidden behind the reserved Beaux Arts façades of the Federal Triangle! The richly embellished interiors of these two landmarks, with their custom-designed aluminum doors, light fixtures, and balustrades, as well as dozens of important Depression-era murals, are not even overshadowed by New York's Rockefeller Center—perhaps the epitome of America's Art Deco development.

Because of the public's lack of understanding of the Art Deco style and even knowledge of the existence of most local Art Deco buildings, a number of important examples, such as the elegant Trans-Lux and Apex theaters, were needlessly razed in the 1970s for commercial development. Others, such as the Greyhound Bus Terminal, were thoughtlessly mutilated. This situation is rapidly changing because of the founding by Richard Striner of the Art Deco Society of Washington in 1982. Through lectures, films, and tours, the Art Deco Society, which has grown enormously in two short years, has been the principal force in focusing attention on our Art Deco heritage. In 1983 the society was successful in lobbying to save the Washington metropolitan area's most significant Art Deco educational building—the Greenbelt Elementary School—from demolition.

Washington Deco conveys the excitement of the new building materials of the age—glass blocks, aluminum, Vitrolite, plastics—as well as of such innovative features as push-button elevators, indirect lighting, and the arrival of air conditioning in the late 1920s. The enormous expansion of the federal government, in order to carry out President Franklin D. Roosevelt's new social programs, resulted in the construction of hundreds of significant buildings to house the growing population. While many major cities experienced little growth during the Great Depression, Washington expanded rapidly both during the 1930s and during World War II to meet the needs of the flood of New Deal and war workers.

Anyone who is interested in the cultural and architectural heritage of the Nation's Capital will benefit from reading this book. The material presented, most of it never published before, adds a missing chapter to the city's rich twentieth-century history. It is greatly to be hoped that *Washington Deco* will be widely read and consulted by local realtors, developers, and entrepreneurs so that the widespread demolition of Art Deco in the 1970s will not be repeated. Indeed, because of a 1981 act of Congress creating tax incentives for the preservation of American landmarks, the future looks bright for the surviving stock of Art Deco buildings. Not only should most of the buildings shown in *Washington Deco* be preserved because of their art and design forms but also because they reflect, more than those of any other era, the spirit of their age. This was the age that saw the arrival of modern technology between the wars, offering rapid and improved transportation, modern urban planning, and better living conditions for the people through the good works of the New Deal. This well-researched volume, with its splendid photographs, successfully reflects this spirit of the new age—through its architects, designers, sculptors, and painters, to whom we all owe a debt of gratitude for leaving us such a rich legacy!

James M. Goode
Smithsonian Institution

PREFACE

This is the first architectural study of Art Deco design in the Nation's Capital. Based on an inventory of approximately 400 structures, it seeks to explore the most significant qualities of Art Deco as it developed in Washington, D.C. In the days when Franklin Roosevelt was President, the sleek, up-to-the-minute designs of Art Deco were merged with the austere classical style of government buildings to create a unique synthesis. And beyond the federal enclave, hundreds of stylish apartment buildings, restaurants, cinemas, and stores brought the Deco spirit to surrounding suburbs. Research for this book was primarily based upon the microfilmed building permits on file at the National Archives, which provided both a chronology and a guide to the most influential Washington architects working in the Deco style in the twenties, thirties, and forties.

A study of Art Deco in the Nation's Capital helps to give a sense of what it felt like to live in the city of *Mr. Smith Goes to Washington*. Poised between its past as a provincial capital and its present as a world urban center, New Deal Washington remains a poignant vision. Art Deco helped to ease the city's transition in symbolic ways, and so its study repays the student of cultural history as much as the student of architecture and design. Consequently, the text for *Washington Deco* seeks to embody a truly interdisciplinary approach to the study of Washington's Art Deco buildings.

In the 1970s, Art Deco was a tenuous presence in Washington, D.C. The Trans-Lux Theater and the Roger Smith Hotel were demolished in 1975, the Apex Theater was demolished in 1977, and the Greyhound Terminal was hidden by a new façade in 1976. Yet, ironically, Art Deco was riding the crest of a major artistic revival that affected almost every facet of American decorative arts.

Several observers noted this fact at the time, but to no avail. Philip Terzian, writing in the *New Republic*, observed that the "lobby and dining room of the Roger Smith were refurbished in 1939 by designer Laurence Emmons in classic art deco, and this gave the place an offhand New Deal ambience that the trendiest of modern night clubs strive . . . to achieve."[1] Gary Wolf, an architectural historian, lamented the fate of the Trans-Lux Theater in the *Washington Post*, observing that just as the theater had once "created a vision of a streamlined future for a depression land of 1937," there remained the "potential for its rebirth as a legitimate movie theatre . . . with space for offices, a restaurant, and shops."[2] And James Goode, the Smithsonian Castle's curator, viewed the destruction of the Trans-Lux and the Apex theaters as the work of "commercial interests who neither appreciated [the buildings'] architectural quality . . . [nor] cared about the public pleas to save them."[3]

All this is beginning to change, however, for a number of entrepreneurs are convinced that Deco design should be preserved in the Nation's Capital. And the founding of the

Art Deco Society of Washington in 1982 provided an additional impetus, one that was directly involved in the saving of Greenbelt Center School from destruction in 1983, when a great outpouring of sentiment persuaded a local board of education to support adaptive use instead of demolition.

Our purpose in describing the Art Deco of Washington is to present the case for preservation. Some believe that Deco was never a significant force in Washington, a misconception we hope to correct in this book. For unlike the consolidated districts of Art Deco to be found in such cities as Miami Beach, in the Nation's Capital Deco buildings are geographically distributed—with the exception of three or four outstanding neighborhood districts—throughout the city and suburbs. This makes Deco a less obvious, but nonetheless pervasive, presence. Not the least of our goals is to reveal the unique and remarkable qualities of Washington's Deco heritage. We will emphasize the best in Washington's Art Deco in our text while providing as complete an inventory as we can in the Appendix.

We wish to thank the following individuals and institutions for their help in preparing this book: Joseph Abel, Elizabeth Allen, Mary E. Allen, the American Institute of Architects Library, the Art Deco Society of Washington, Roy Ashwood, Randee Bernstein, Beverly Brannan, Jack Brince, Raymond Burkett, Stephanie Byrnes, the Columbia Historical Society, Sherry Cucchiella, Oscar De Lima, Tracy Dillard, Dimock Gallery, Theodore Dominick, Don't Tear It Down, Jane Dougherty, Perry Fisher, Jody Gebhardt, James Goode, Wendy Goldberg, Kent Griffiths, Robert Headley, Norma Hendershott, Lynne Heneson, Mary Ison, Karen Jaehne, Larry Kanter, Granville Klink, Dorothy Lauber, Edwin Lawless, Glenn Leiner, the Library of Congress Prints and Photographs Division, Richard Longstreth, Maxwell MacKenzie, James Maher, Margaret Mankin, Jack Masarsky, Joyce McDonald, Eileen McGuckian, Pamela Mickley, Lenore Miller, the National Archives, John Pearce, C. Ford Peatross, Ellen E. Powers, Leslie Rainer, Parris Rizzo, Gail Rothrock, James Sweeney, Eleanor Snyder, Mary Ternes, Florian Thayn, Tony Vasaio, Alan Virta, the Washington Chapter of A.I.A., W. Waverly Webb, Jesse Weinstein, Richard Guy Wilson, and Karel Yasko.

I

THE SPIRIT OF ART DECO

It emerged from the 1925 Paris exposition of the decorative-industrial arts. Unfettered by an orthodox creed, it was a link between the avant-garde, the industrial designers, and the mass-consumption culture of the 1920s and 1930s. Art Deco is a style representing the daydreams of an age: the Chrysler Building with its gleaming pinnacle of stainless steel terraces; the future metropolis envisioned by the filmmaker Fritz Lang and by the artist Hugh Ferriss; swanky apartments with stylish objects of black and green onyx and blue-tinted glass. Art Deco was the streamlined locomotive designs of Raymond Loewy, the huge clipper planes, and the ocean liners of Norman Bel Geddes. It was the architecture of Vitrolite, of aluminum, and of glass brick. It was the Emerald City of Oz and the World's Fairs of 1933 and 1939.

The sources of Art Deco can be traced to the turn of the century: Art Nouveau, Vienna Secession, and modernist movements in painting were all among the very early inspirations of Art Deco design. These sources and inspirations were fused in 1925 in an international exposition in Paris, the Exposition Internationale des Arts Décoratifs et Industriels Modernes, from which abbreviations like "Art Deco" and "Art Moderne" would be drawn. This exposition had been planned for years as the latest in a series of design fairs. The 1925 exposition featured works by acclaimed masters, such as the cabinetwork of Ruhlmann and the silverwork of Puiforcat: works that would set the standard for elegance throughout the twenties and thirties. The ornate, jazzy motifs introduced at Paris in 1925 would filter down into popular culture to the level of dime-store glitter. Whatever the differences in scholarly appraisals of Art Deco, everyone seems to agree that the 1925 show was the focal point of the movement.

Otherwise, however, scholars disagree about the proper definition of the style. Some, like the British art historian Bevis Hillier, have used the term to describe the broadest possible range of decorative arts in the twenties and thirties. Others, like the architectural historian David Gebhard, have taken the position that the jazzy look of the 1925 show was supplanted in the thirties by something different, a streamlined style inspired by the works of industrial designers rather than Parisian craftsmen.[1] Some have referred to the streamlined style of the thirties as "Art Moderne" or "Streamlined Moderne." "Moderne," indeed, was the commonest term to describe the most up-to-the-minute designs of the twenties and thirties, while "Art Deco" was an abbreviation introduced in 1966 at a retrospective exhibition at the Musée des Arts Décoratifs in Paris. The term was used by Bevis Hillier in 1968 as the title for the first book on the subject. It quickly caught on with the connoisseurs—though a number of scholars disagreed about its range.

Both the jazzy look of the 1925 show and the streamlined style of the thirties, in fact, were part of a broader design spectrum. At the two extremes of the spectrum were the radically functional styles, devoid of ornamentation, and the openly traditionalistic styles, such as classical. If anything, Art Deco was a middle path between the two antithetical extremes. And this, we believe, provides the soundest basis for defining and expounding the style.

For all the diversity confronting designers in the 1920s and 1930s, the feud between the radical modernists—whose principles were known as the "International Style" by the early 1930s—and defenders of traditional style became the point of departure. In a way, both the radical apostles of functionalism and the guardians of classical verities were reacting against the extremely ornate decorations of Victorian designers in favor of "cleaner" lines. But otherwise, they differed completely, and polemical exchanges were bitter. "The styles are a lie," was the famous 1923 maxim of Le Corbusier: away with decorative artifice in favor of functional "honesty." The wave of the future was the rational "mass-production spirit. The spirit of constructing mass-production houses. The spirit of living in mass-production houses."[2] The architect George Howe was much more severe when he argued in 1930 that "the overwhelming majority" of traditionalistic structures produced at the same time were "ramshackle, sentimental, pretentious, dishonest and ugly. . . ."[3] The International Style, of which he approved, prided itself on the maxim "Form Follows Function." In truth, it represented an amalgam of modern styles, from the German Bauhaus to the works of Le Corbusier. The common theme was a radically severe lack of embellishment or softening features.

The traditionalists—usually adherents of the classical formulas—responded with derision. *The Federal Architect* in 1930 reflected on the "deadly germ" of modern architecture, "propagating like the Japanese beetle in obscene profusion. . . ."[4] Ralph T. Walker, an important practitioner who championed the use of architectural ornamentation, lamented that "the European architect is so engrossed with the two dimensions of Euclidean geometry and a theory of structure, that he has ceased to produce architecture for human beings."[5] Traditionalists rallied to a classical revival, one that had been building since the 1890s. Twentieth-century architects like Bertram Goodhue and Paul Philippe Cret pioneered a modernized classical look that would reach its zenith in the 1930s as a far more universally accepted international style than the creed of radical functionalism.[6] It became, indeed, something close to the official government architecture around the world and it powerfully influenced the building of New Deal Washington. The most popular term for this style is "stripped classical."

Between these embittered extremes, the Art Deco designers cut a jaunty path indeed, unhindered by an ideology. Rejecting any orthodox strictures, Deco designers felt free to assimilate any motifs that expressed the spirit of the age. In the search for elegance and chic, the Deco spirit could borrow from the International Style and blend it, to the horrified gaze of its supporters, with exotic and ancient motifs, notably Egyptian and Aztec. The goal was to capture the haunting savor of life in the Jazz Age. This answered implicitly a longing expressed by Frank Lloyd Wright in 1930. Beyond the mere "sentimentality of the 'ornamental,' " he declared, and the newer "sterility of 'ornaphobia,' " the creative artist should be driven to achieve "romance."[7] What better, more evocative description of Art Deco's appeal? The Chrysler Building, with its jazzy and somewhat eccentric commercial flair, might not, of course, have been exactly what Wright had in mind, but the movement it represented was prompted by longings that were similar to those expressed by the master.

These longings were also at work in the streamline style of the thirties. Like the spirit of the Paris exposition of 1925, the aesthetics of streamlining was an effort to express the spirit of the age—and without ideology. The emphasis on cleanness and smoothness, to be sure, was closely related to the International Style's machine aesthetics. But the streamline vogue of the 1930s went far beyond any functional basis and became yet

This extraordinary Art Deco bar, added to the older Carlton Hotel in the early 1930s, admirably illustrates the Deco spirit of the twenties and thirties. Such interiors as this one show that the Deco spirit was rich in elements linking the moods of the two decades. (Courtesy Theodor Horydczak Collection, Library of Congress Prints and Photographs Division)

another expressive and decorative idiom applied to almost any conceivable object, whether functionally justified or not. Streamlining—though a functional imperative of speed that was justified in vehicles to cut wind-resistance—made little engineering sense when applied to a stationary object or building. It was simply the "smart," nautical, or rakish look that counted more than anything else in the thirties.

Rather than severely separating the Deco style of the twenties from the streamline style of the thirties, we feel that they both represented discernible, related trends within a broader decorative movement, in which they overlapped. This latter point deserves emphasis: for proliferating studies of 1930s design reveal a wealth of structures where the streamline style and the ornate motifs of the 1925 Paris show were very thoroughly and totally combined. This is true of the district in South Miami Beach, developed in the late thirties and early forties, that was added to the National Register of Historic Places in 1979 as an Art Deco district. It is true of such landmark 1930s structures as the Cincinnati Union Terminal (1933) and the annex built for the Library of Congress in Washington (1935–39). It is true of 1930s apartment buildings and movie palaces throughout Washington. As Hillier emphasized in 1971, "the art of the twenties was not suddenly snuffed out in 1930 with a magician's 'Now you see it, now you don't. . . .' There was a strong continuity."[8]

The Deco-streamline continuum represented the broad middle ground of design in the twenties and thirties. It could often shade over into hybrid combinations with the International Style on the one extreme or with the stripped classical style on the other. It is not, therefore, uniformly easy to define where it begins and ends. But the difficulty can at times be the source of whimsy and good sport. A very charming phrase, for example, to refer to the hybrid combinations of Art Deco and stripped classical so commonly found in Washington was recently coined by historian James Goode: Greco-Deco!

Throughout this work, consequently, Art Deco, though a retrospective term, will be used to refer to the broad mediation and synthesis, the flowing design continuum, the middle ground of design in both the 1920s and 1930s. The movement given momentum by the 1925 Paris exposition continued throughout the thirties, adding and assimilating voguish trends like the streamline style in an effort to be "up-to-the-minute," to express the spirit of the age in both elegant and playful moods, and to serve as a symbolic fusion of past and future in the present.

All of the styles of the twenties and thirties, from the International Style to Art Deco to the stripped classical style, were in part responses to the cultural traumas created by the devastation of World War I, though all had roots in artistic movements before the war. As Roland Stromberg has said, the war, for many, triggered "a sort of apocalyptic, Nietzschean mood which saw in this catastrophe both an awful judgement on a doomed civilization and a necessary prelude to a complete rebirth."9 This mood was the basis for many of the classic literary works of the twenties, from Oswald Spengler's *Decline of the West* to T.S. Eliot's *The Waste Land* to D.H. Lawrence's search for the primal wellsprings of human creativity to Arnold Toynbee's attempt to delineate historical cycles of decline and fall.

In an age when artistic spirits were flirting with the notion that Western culture was approaching the end of a cycle, Art Deco was a means of reaching out to the two extremes of the historical continuum, the ancient past and the distant future, and of fusing fact and fantasy. Hence the familiar Deco evocations in the twenties of Aztec gods in Buck Rogers settings. If the West was really in decline, after all, then what was likely to replace it? A resurgence of atavistic forces? Nature worship, or the force of the libido, as D.H. Lawrence implied? A machine culture based upon "L'Esprit Nouveau" or the anti-utopia of Aldous Huxley's *Brave New World*? By conjuring both with the remote past and with the distant future in the same designs, Art Deco was perhaps an attempt to "locate" the modern world in a broader pattern of meaning.

Hillier has frequently noted that the zigzag look of the 1920s in Art Deco represented not only the rhythms of jazz but also the imagery of Aztec and Mayan art. Next to ancient Egyptian motifs (made suddenly the rage by the opening of King Tutankhamen's tomb) and the neoclassical revival, the popularity of Aztec-derived motifs in the twenties was the notable feature of a vogue for ancient cultures. One sensed the return of strange gods when beholding the terraced buildings of the twenties or the visions of the illustrator Hugh Ferriss in his book *The Metropolis of Tomorrow*: skyscrapers like Aztec pyramids stretched to the height of industrial-age towers.

This was the spirit of Art Deco between 1925 and 1930. While America was not represented with an actual exhibit at the Paris show, an American delegation was sent by Herbert Hoover, who was then serving as Secretary of Commerce. The purpose was to keep American business apprised of marketing trends, and Art Deco was adopted as the latest vogue by department stores like Saks Fifth Avenue and Lord & Taylor. Architects adopted it, too: Joseph Urban, Raymond Hood, Ely Jacques Kahn, and William Van Alen (the designer of the Chrysler Building) were among the foremost architects during the 1920s to adopt the principles of Art Deco in America. These principles were never announced to the world with a publicist's flair, but the clear intent of the Deco

Floating goddess crowns the Carlton Hotel bar, in which, evidently, the bartender sat concealed. Though the Carlton Hotel was designed by Mihran Mesrobian, the designer of the Deco bar and lounge remains unknown. (Courtesy Theodor Horydczak Collection, Library of Congress)

designers was to utilize decoration as symbolism, as a means of conjuring with modern hopes and fears.

The ancient past and the distant future were temporal points of comparison, as we have seen. Symbols of nature and the machine were another form of polarity—and synthesis. Zigzag forms suggested the force of electrical power, both chained and free:

the thunderbolt as well as the harnessed power of the dynamo. Plant, sun, and cloud motifs were among the other nature symbols adapted to Art Deco. At the Chrysler Building's spire, tiers of triangular windows gestured up to the heavens in a way that suggested sunrays, but the terraces also suggested the interlocking of gears.

The 1920s, of course, were years of heedless frivolity, at least superficially. Art Deco reflected this in its use of bright materials and colors that approached the point of luridness. While the style matured somewhat in the 1930s, these were years of abandon. The fountain was a typical sign of the times, as Hillier has said:

> The symbols of the twenties [were] innocuous. . . . apart from the iridescent bubble about to burst, the most popular motif was the fountain, spilling its waters wantonly, unrecantably, and with a musical tinkle. . . . The disillusioned man dreams of regeneration in the fountains of Sans Souci.[10]

And Eliot's *Waste Land* (albeit in a chastening manner) had also played upon the theme of water-redemption in a world of broken values. But in 1929 the fountain of the twenties, whatever its powers for redemption or dissipation, gave way to the drought-stricken world of Depression and Hooverville.

The first reaction for many was to cling to what was destroyed—"Happy Days Are Here Again." But very rapidly, culture began to take on a more serious tone. By 1933, the Great Depression was seen as a providential curse—as a lesson for a wayward people. It was also viewed as a challenge to the social pioneer. The cynics, the disillusioned, and the various profligates of the twenties were now swept aside in the surge of desire to rebuild a new world. The goal was to master industrial culture—to bring irrigation to a parched land, though not through the wanton caprice of a bubbling fountain, but rather through engineering, through rational public works. Donald J. Bush has traced the effects of this mood upon the decorative arts:

> The open car associated with the reckless pace of the Roaring Twenties gave way to the closed car of the thirties, a vehicle better suited to efficiency than to wild abandon. Frivolity in the decorative arts was discarded for symbols of sensible economy.[11]

The result was at times austere, but seldom forbidding. For however bleak the Depression could be, the goal of a secure future prompted an almost utopian release of spirit. In their book *Art and the Machine*, Sheldon and Martha Cheney declared in 1936:

> Already we can glimpse the community of tomorrow as a place unified and harmonious: an industrially-designed machine-age entity . . . It is the emergent product of the twentieth-century industrial pioneers: a new American scene, coordinated, artist-determined, machine-realized.[12]

This was how the streamlining vogue burst forth in the United States. In a stagnant economy, streamlining offered both a symbolic means of escape, through its imagery of speed, and a symbolic control of unruly economic events through the "smooth" coordination of planning. A new breed of industrial designers—men like Raymond Loewy, Donald Deskey, and Norman Bel Geddes—infused the spirit of the decorative arts with the worship of crisp, sleek lines.[13] As early as 1930, Frank Lloyd Wright had proclaimed that "today, it seems to me, we hear this cry 'Be Clean' from the depths of our own need. It is almost as though the Machine itself had, by force, issued edict similar to Shinto— 'Be Clean.' Clean lines . . . clean purposes."[14] The Cheneys, too, took delight in the spectacle of "lonely gadgets and humps and unsightly pipes" being "brought within the unified scheme," because the heedless twenties had now given way to the master plan and the social engineer.[15]

Norman Bel Geddes, in his book *Horizons*—a title to conjure with—made clear the degree to which designers were aware of such political and social issues:[16] a new order— a humane and rational world. Much of this seemed to be a link to the same democratic spirit present in books like Carl Sandburg's *The People, Yes*. In the town of Greenbelt,

Maryland—a New Deal showcase of urban planning—what one resident termed the "windswept" lines of the buildings expressed the idealistic yearnings. The streamlined façade of the Greenbelt Center Elementary School is punctuated with bas-relief sculptures of common men: staunch, heroic pioneers.

Yet the image of a new dawn could hold sinister potential in the 1930s, as events in Europe proved. Crisp lines, neoclassical precision, and symbols of clean and unified order could lead in the direction spelled out by Hillier when he says that Art Deco motifs of the thirties were "more dynamic" than those of the twenties:

. . . rising sun, racing clouds, and hair streaming in the wind. These, too, were mnemonics, like fascist slogans. They are associated with Herrenvolk, youth movements, and Nordic nudes gambolling under a blonde Aryan sun.[17]

The outdoor sculptures of American Art Deco in its 1930s phase are not, one has to admit, completely removed from the styles of the German heroic sculptures by Arno Breker and Josef Thorak, nor is the neoclassical character of some of its buildings completely distinct from the creations of the official Third Reich architect, Albert Speer.[18] But beyond this, comparisons cannot be ventured. Whatever the fears of people like Sinclair Lewis, whose 1936 novel, *It Can't Happen Here*, envisioned a fascist America, American Art Deco, as American culture generally, remained overwhelmingly benign in the years of Franklin Roosevelt.

In fact, in the manner of the Swing musician who punned that he would rather have American youth "hailing the band leader than heiling the Bund leader," Art Deco designs were generally a source of cosmopolitanism: the youthfulness of Radio City Music Hall, the inspiring elegance of the Fred Astaire and Ginger Rogers dance settings, the tacky pleasures of five-and-dime jewelry, neon lighting and glass-bricked entranceways, the exotic coral-hued hotels of Miami Beach in the late 1930s, and the abundant Latin and jazz influences—most of which were light years away from Wagnerian imagery.

Whatever the political or social content of Art Deco, however, streamlining, with its sense of both control and of protean power-through-speed, was the style's apotheosis. Through streamlining, the skyscraper vogue of the twenties eventually yielded to horizontality. Bus terminals across the country and sleek aluminum diners reflected this. Perhaps inspired by the ocean liners of Norman Bel Geddes—which were never constructed though one was featured in the film *The Big Broadcast of 1938*—a nautical flavor infused the designs of thirties' Art Deco. The Trans-Lux Theater in Washington, D.C., and the Coca-Cola bottling plant in Los Angeles spread the vogue, even (in the case of the latter) down to the use of portholes.

In both its serious and playful moods, Art Deco had reached its zenith in 1939, the year of New York World's Fair, with its Trylon and Perisphere. The enduring monuments—the Chrysler and Empire State buildings, the Golden Gate Bridge, Rockefeller Center, and the Waldorf-Astoria—were already considered classics. But while a number of derivative tendencies persisted into the late 1940s and 1950s, war disrupted the style's development. Art Deco had been chic, but in the aftermath of war, the American designer wished to be modern, not "moderne." The International Style was on the ascendancy in the world of corporate business, and once a period of gaudy exuberance had passed in the fifties—the tail-fin era—the middle class settled down to the low-key styles of Danish modern and ranch-house suburbia. These were years in which Art Deco was ignored, rejected, or considered expendable.

The revival began in the mid-1960s. From the realm of "kitsch," Art Deco was admitted to the canons of "camp." Revivals of period movies, the writings of Hillier and David Gebhard, and the important exhibition at the Minneapolis Institute of Arts in 1971, raised the style from oblivion. Influential, too, was a sea-change in the world of urban

A mischievous mood is achieved by the use of mock flames, executed in neon, in the fireplace adorning the Carlton Hotel lounge. The photographer, Theodor Horydczak, was one of the preeminent commercial photographers in Washington during the twenties, thirties, and forties. (Courtesy Theodor Horydczak Collection, Library of Congress)

planning and the "Post-Modernist" movement in architecture. Most recently, the designation of an Art Deco historic district in Miami Beach by the National Register, along with the effort to save Radio City Music Hall, the restoration of the Chrysler Building, and the brisk trade in antiques related to Art Deco, have revealed that the style is at last legitimate.

Despite the resurgence of interest in design of the twenties and thirties, however, Art Deco architecture remains threatened. The validity of Art Deco as a mature and original style, its merit as a significant phase of twentieth-century design, and its unique characteristics as a contribution to American building arts, are still not sufficiently recognized. It confirms the truism that every new style requires at least two generations for its qualities to be acknowledged. The increasing rate of demolition of buildings from the twenties and thirties indicates that preservation strategies are needed quickly. Only with an adequate inventory of each city's Deco buildings—like those already carried out, with varying degrees of thoroughness, in New York City, Miami Beach, Los Angeles, and Tulsa—can we hope to preserve the enduring spirit of Art Deco in America.

2
WASHINGTON CULTURE IN THE YEARS OF ART DECO

The crusading spirit of World War I was over, and President Wilson had departed. President Calvin Coolidge proclaimed that "the business of America is business." Idealism had fled amid the culture of the "Roaring '20s." Yet Americans continued to search for heroes like Charles Lindbergh. With the 1928 election victory of Herbert Hoover, a sense of inspiration returned. A professional administrator, Hoover had masterminded the enormous American relief efforts in Europe at the close of World War I. Americans looked to him as a humanitarian figure with the expertise to provide prosperity for all. Hoover himself looked forward to the dawn of a "new era" when poverty would be abolished.

To be sure, the imminent stock market crash soon belied such faith, but the most serious effects of the crash took some time to develop. Thus, in 1930, Washingtonians could sense that the coarser aspects of the twenties were yielding to a serious-minded and elegant new society.

The elegance seemed to be reflected in buildings like the Shoreham and the Westchester hotels, both completed in 1930, the former designed by Joseph Abel and the latter designed by Harvey Warwick, who lived in the building for many years. The earliest traces of Art Deco were now filtering into Washington, mixing with Gothic, classical, and Renaissance-revival touches. Above all, Art Deco would merge with the powerful Washington tradition of classical architecture.

The tradition, bequeathed from the days of L'Enfant, Latrobe, and Mills, had been given a new infusion since the turn of the century. Inspired by the "City Beautiful" movement, the guardians of Washington's aesthetics attempted to enthrone the classical impulse. The influential McMillan Commission, whose plans were entrusted to the oversight of a Commission of Fine Arts in 1910, provided suitable recommendations on public buildings and parkland. By the early twenties, the completion of the Lincoln Memorial, designed by Henry Bacon, and the National Academy of Science building, designed by Bertram Goodhue, served as important milestones in a wave of classical building that would last through the early-to-mid-1940s.

Accordingly, the seriousness of the Hoover era found expression in plans for the new "Federal Triangle." Actually, the plans to create a federal office district between Constitution and Pennsylvania avenues dated to the turn of the century.[1] Congressional authorization arrived in 1926, and construction began in 1928. Fortuitous trends made the early Triangle buildings reflect the spirit of the Hoover era, the spirit that Lois Craig has described in terms of "forbidding stone temples engraved with solemn quotations, landscaped with automobiles and bristling with guards":[2] a suitable form of design when the stiff and forbidding "Hoover collar" was the height of fashion for conservative dressers.

This early entertainment lounge in the Shoreham Hotel (circa 1930) shows important stylistic combinations of Art Deco and classicism. The architect, Joseph Abel, employed variations of the Greek-Key pattern throughout the hotel, as can still be seen in the lighting fixtures of the promenade "Birdcage Walk." (Courtesy Theodor Horydczak Collection, Library of Congress).

The construction of the Federal Triangle was performed by the Public Buildings Commission, with final authority vested in the Secretary of the Treasury, Andrew Mellon, and the Supervising Architect of the Treasury Department, Louis A. Simon. Under plans proposed by the president of the American Institute of Architects, Milton B. Medary, Secretary Mellon selected a board of architectural consultants to plan the massive development, with each member of the board to be responsible for designing a particular building, to avoid monotony.[3] The board was headed by Edward H. Bennett.[4]

While the Federal Triangle buildings possessed the individuality Medary hoped for, they powerfully reflected the classical impulse in Washington, but now combined with important traces of Art Deco. They reflected the firm conviction among the arbiters of taste that the dignified forms bequeathed from the late eighteenth and early nineteenth centuries should be preserved in new construction—with the corollary commitments to discard the most extreme Victorian departures from classicism and to guard against extreme forms of modernism: in short, against the International Style. So cohesive a group were the architects and planners of federal buildings that in 1927 they formed the Association of Federal Architects. In 1930 they began to publish a magazine, *The Federal Architect*, which served as a forum on issues of architectural taste.

Federal architects were frequently accused of being rigid "traditionalists," a charge with occasional truth. But in their own defense they claimed to be no more rigid than the modernists who insisted on function stripped of ornament.

In 1933 the architect Paul Cret attacked the "ballyhoo" of the "left wing of the modernists," claiming for himself the right "to do what I believe is appropriate even if somebody else did it before me."[5] And in 1930 an editorial in *The Federal Architect* condemning "the germ of Modern Architecture," with its "thumb-nosing at the past," nonetheless reserved the right to be pleasantly surprised by any new approaches to design that could synthesize past and present. "Believe it or not," the editorial writer admitted, "modern architecture can be good," but he hastened to add that this meant both "a breaking away from the old architecture" and "a loyalty to it"; in other words, "the Moderne traditionalized, the Traditional modernized."[6]

The result was what Lois Craig and others have called "starved classicism" or "stripped classicism." Perhaps the finest example of this is the building designed by Paul Cret for the Folger Shakespeare Library of 1932. Its flowing lines are a twentieth-century restatement of ancient themes. But throughout the classical structures designed by Cret, by John Russell Pope, and by other philosophically congenial architects during the thirties, the motifs of the 1925 Parisian exposition could be sensed. To a large extent, the spirit of Art Deco fulfilled the classicists' desire for the "Moderne traditionalized, the traditional modernized" (as its jazzier forms fulfilled, implicitly, the longing of Frank Lloyd Wright for "romance" in design). This does not imply that all classical buildings of the 1930s in Washington had Art Deco elements, but the "Greco-Deco" classification of James Goode provides an apposite term for this fusion.

Hoover, of course, was doomed by the worsening effects of the stock market crash, effects that were gradually producing America's worst depression. Washington, with its civil servants comprising so much of the work force, suffered much less than other cities, but the true extent of the nation's economic plight was made vivid by 1932. The famous march of the "Bonus Army," a protesting group of unemployed veterans of World War I, brought thousands of marchers to Washington demanding congressional payment of veterans' benefits years before they were due. Though initially handled with grace by the superintendent of police, the marchers became such a source of fear to the President that suddenly the Army was called out. In a sad chapter of their early careers, both Douglas MacArthur and Dwight D. Eisenhower had to lead their troops to the marchers' Anacostia shantytown—the shanties were burned and the marchers were evicted with tear gas.

None of this did much for the fortunes of Hoover, when a quarter of America's work force was unemployed and when people were suddenly reduced to living in grim communities of barrels and cardboard boxes. "Brother Can You Spare a Dime" was the ditty that Bing Crosby and Rudy Vallee were crooning in 1932, the year Hoover was thrown out of office.

What followed can hardly be imagined by those who have never experienced a major social crisis. Though historians for years have pointed out that the rhetoric of Franklin Delano Roosevelt's inspiring first inaugural address was followed by contradictory policies, what the President pledged was precisely the "bold, persistent experimentation" that was probably needed in a time of unprecedented problems. In an instant, Washington became the "nerve center" of the country. "In the spring of 1933," writes William Leuchtenburg, "Washington quickened to the feverish pace of the new mobilization. From state agricultural colleges and university campuses, from law faculties and social work schools, the young men flocked to Washington to take part in the new mobilization. Wholly apart from their beliefs or special competences, they imparted an enormous energy to the business of governing and impressed almost everyone with their contagious high spirits. . . ."[7] A more pungent view was presented in George Peek's recollection of "the plague of young lawyers" who "settled on Washington," claiming to be "friends of somebody or other and mostly of Felix Frankfurter and Jerome Frank. They floated airily into offices, took desks, asked for papers and found no end of things to be busy about. I never found out why they came, what they did or why they left."[8]

This was the Washington of Thomas Corcoran and Benjamin Cohen, of Harry Hopkins and Harold Ickes—and of Senator Huey Long. From the desks of the "Brain Trusters" came the welter of "alphabet agencies" chartered to administer relief and to promote rebuilding—the CCC and the WPA, the AAA, the TVA, and the PWA.[9] The Roosevelt era was characterized by a sense of both retrenchment and pioneering: an attempt to conserve America's broader continuities by keeping pace with the times. Against the chaos bred by conservative laissez-faire was to be fashioned a conserving liberal order, as Leuchtenburg says:

The New Dealers . . . had their Heavenly City: the greenbelt town, clean, green, and white, with children playing in light, airy, spacious schools: the government project at Longview, Washington, with small houses, each of different design, colored roofs, and gardens of flowers and vegetables; the Mormon villages of Utah that M.L. Wilson kept in his mind's eye—immaculate farmsteads on broad, rectangular streets; most of all, the Tennessee Valley, with its model town of Norris, the tall transmission towers, the white dams, the glistening wire strands, the valley where "a vision of villages and clean small factories has been growing into the minds of thoughtful men." Scandinavia was their model abroad, not only because it summoned up images of the countryside of Denmark . . . but because it represented the "middle way" of happy accommodation of public and private institutions the New Deal sought to achieve.[10]

The nerve center to coordinate this vision of regional redevelopment was Washington. Its role was symbolized in images of eagles and thunderbolts: the paraphernalia of mobilization was everywhere apparent, especially in terminology. Young men went forth to reforest America's desolate regions in a new "Civilian Conservation Corps." In the *Architectural Forum* were schematic charts showing "Washington's Building Battalion": some twenty-eight different federal agencies and programs affecting construction and building. Members of the "Building Battalion" were frequently put to work in wooden temporary structures left over from World War I on Washington's Mall.

Others were quartered, ironically, in vacant mansions in Georgetown or in the neighborhood of Dupont Circle, mansions the rich were abandoning in favor of homes being built uptown in the new developments of Wesley Heights and Spring Valley. In one such mansion, Rexford Guy Tugwell and planners from the Agriculture Department's Resettlement Administration conceived the program of "greenbelt cities" they hoped would be a model for America's suburbanization—model towns to both absorb the flow of impoverished migrants and to demonstrate how the virtues of city and country life could be combined through benevolent planning.

In all, Washington's population grew by 36 percent in the thirties, while every other major city except Los Angeles lost residents.[11] The reason was obvious enough, and in 1939, Edwin Rosskam spoke of the city's "nameless horde with civil service rating," a horde he believed accounted for half of the city's residents:

The Federal Government is the destiny of Washington, D.C. Here almost everybody either works for the government, depends on somebody who works for the government, works for somebody who works for the government, or is trying to sell something to somebody who works for the government.[12]

Rosskam believed that the majority of the new arrivals had small town antecedents, "which accounts for some of the provincial aspects of our cosmopolitan capital," along with its transience: "Washington has more boarding houses and bath-sharing apartments than any other city of comparable size."[13]

The youthful spirit of New Deal Washington was represented in the Hollywood caperings of bashful Jimmy Stewart and insouciant Jean Arthur in the film classic of 1939,

The façade of the Keystone Restaurant at 1223 Good Hope Rd., SE, was executed in the plate glass known as "Vitrolite." Neighborhood restaurants like this one abounded in New Deal Washington. (Courtesy Theodor Horydczak Collection, Library of Congress)

A typical Deco storefront added to an older building in the 1930s: the Merry-Land Club (now defunct) at 1405 L Street, NW. Very few of these street-level Deco façades have survived more recent waves of modernization. (Courtesy Theodor Horydczak Collection, Library of Congress)

Curb service was a popular feature at the Hot Shoppes restaurants in the forties and afterwards. The period features of the surviving Hot Shoppes have long been lost to the never-ending design-metamorphoses of mass-merchandising. (Photo by John Collier, courtesy Farm Security Administration Collection, Library of Congress Prints and Photographs Division)

The Silver Fox was a popular restaurant and lounge on Wisconsin Avenue below the District of Columbia line in Friendship Heights. The streamlined façade was added in the mid-forties, only to be swept away in the early 1970s by a huge shopping mall. (Courtesy Theodor Horydczak Collection, Library of Congress)

The spirit of roadside America during the late 1930s was reflected in refreshment stands like this one in Berwyn Heights, Maryland. Vernacular design, considered expendable when brand-new, becomes increasingly valuable with age as a link to cultural history. (Photo by Jack Delano, courtesy Farm Security Administration Collection, Library of Congress)

Mr. Smith Goes to Washington," with its tough-guy reporters won over in the end to the freshness and idealistic fervor of provincials like "Jefferson Smith."

The youthful spirit of Washington was modernistic and "smart." One can almost hear "swing" music while gazing at surviving photographs of young men in white linen suits and women in their modish calf-length dresses and sloping hats, departing from federal offices in taxis or in streetcars, bound, perhaps, for a newsreel showing at the Trans-Lux Theater of a speech by President Roosevelt, or for the elegant new high-rise apartments of Connecticut Avenue or Sixteenth Street with their stylish glass-bricked entranceways and their stainless-steel trim. This was the scene in which Art Deco became vogue in the Nation's Capital—the era of sleek "Moderne."

In government building, the vogue was reflected in the Federal Triangle. The Justice Department and Federal Trade Commission buildings abounded with Deco features—

The utopian spirit of Greenbelt typified the New Deal vision of garden communities: a pioneering effort to replace the alleged chaos of sprawling cities with a new, "streamlined" balance of city and country living. (Photo by Marion Post Wolcott, courtesy Farm Security Administration Collection, Library of Congress)

as did the annex to the Library of Congress completed in 1939 and named for Thomas Jefferson.[14]

Throughout these buildings, the presence of New Deal values was perpetuated in public art. Though much of the federal art of the thirties is popularly known as "WPA art," a great deal of it was actually channelled through the Treasury Department's Public Works of Art Project (PWAP), succeeded by the department's Fine Arts Section, headed by Edward Bruce. Through programs like these, the murals of Harold Weston, William Gropper, and painters of the "social realist" school were made a part of the New Deal legacy. With their scenes of common men as the builders of a new society—and with occasional notes of social protest that approached the point of surrealism, especially in the murals adorning the Justice Department building—the spirit of the murals existed in the same uneasy relation to the "smartness" of youthful Washington as did the Hollywood situations contrived for Frank Capra's films. The interplay between social realist art and the voguish appeal of Art Deco was a fitting commentary on a land diverse enough to encompass both the ritziness of Fred Astaire and Cary Grant and the homely directness of Woody Guthrie and the "folkishness" of Aaron Copland's music.

The *pièce de resistance* of federal Art Deco in New Deal Washington was Greenbelt, the model town in the Maryland suburbs designed by the planners of the Agriculture Department's Resettlement Administration. From an original list of 100 cities that seemed to merit the development of greenbelt satellite towns as havens for the settlement and retraining of rural migrants, only three cities, Washington, Milwaukee, and Cincinnati, were selected. The project was limited by budget restrictions and court decisions that challenged its constitutionality.[15] Greenbelt, Maryland, Greendale, Wisconsin, and Greenhills, Ohio, were pushed to completion, while the project of Greenbrook, New

In contrast to the feisty commercial spirit of roadside development, this domestic scene reflects the ideals of the planned community of Greenbelt, Maryland. Federal planners hoped that the "Green Towns" program would help to encourage an orderly suburbanization with tidy commercial enclaves built in central pedestrian malls surrounded by lush greenery. (Photo by Marjory Collins, courtesy Office of War Information Collection, Library of Congress)

Jersey, was opposed by local residents.

Greenbelt, Maryland, was built between 1936 and 1937, and its first residents were lower-middle-class families. Their spirit may be gleaned from the dedication address, "We Pioneers," that was published in the *Greenbelt Cooperator*, the town's first newspaper, in 1937. The author was Mary E. Van Cleave:

Let us keep ourselves, our community, our city government, our ideals, as clean as our new, windswept roofs. Let us conduct ourselves and the management of our Greenbelt in such a way as to deserve the pride with which all America will be looking on. We who have been endowed with the greatest living heritage on earth by our ancestors still have that hardiness and determination underneath. Greenbelt will be a success, with the cooperation of her citizens and with the help of God.[16]

Greenbelt followed the curves of a crescent-shaped ridge, and the houses were clustered according to the lay of the land. The town center was designed with a pedestrian mall and pedestrian underpasses, but parking was arranged in the familiar "Main Street" pattern of American small towns. The sweeping lines of the theater and stores at the town center were modest in spirit, as was the more flamboyant Deco-influenced Greenbelt Center School. The outlying housing units were a mixture of Art Deco (especially in their use of glass brick) and the spare lines of the International Style. The Center School, with its steamlined entrance, its white façade with "aerodynamic" struts, and its bas-relief sculptures of common men, remains a stunning architectural vision of crisp, utopian design.

Other approaches to low-cost housing in Washington were based upon the new authority of the Federal Housing Administration (FHA) to insure loans, an authority that several astute developers, notably Gustave Ring, the developer of Arlington's Colonial Village,

End-of-the-decade elegance: the lobby of the Roger Smith Hotel as redesigned by Laurence Emmons in 1939. The use of the classical Greek-Key motif, in both the mezzanine railing and the carpet pattern, is evident. Formerly the Hotel Powhatan, the building was acquired by the New York-based Roger Smith corporation in the 1930s. The building, lobby and all, was demolished in 1975; nothing was saved. (Courtesy Roger Smith Corporation)

used to create an area-wide network of garden apartments, many of which were important contributions to the heritage of Art Deco. More serious housing problems were addressed by Washington's Alley Dwelling Authority, created by Congress in 1934 to help the District of Columbia rid itself of thousands of slums and replace them with public housing. While Washington remained a "Jim Crow" city in the 1930s, such projects were a slight contribution to improving race relations, as was the symbolic intercession of Eleanor Roosevelt and Harold Ickes to help the black contralto Marian Anderson perform at the Lincoln Memorial after the Daughters of the American Revolution refused to let her perform at Constitution Hall.

That was in 1939. Very soon, the approach of another world war would bring overwhelming changes to Washington—new temporary structures on the Mall, the colossal building that would soon become known as the Pentagon, and a gradual shift to more severe applications of modern design that seemed, somehow, more in keeping with a grim age. Deco would linger for a while, in the myriad garden apartments that continued to be produced to accommodate an ever-burgeoning populace, and even in the lines of the new National Airport. But the coming architectural destiny of Washington was shown in structures like William Lescaze's Longfellow Building at 1741 Rhode Island Avenue, NW, and in the terms of the controversial competition for design of a new Smithsonian Gallery of Art, a competition won by the team of Eliel and Eero Saarinen and Robert Swanson in 1939 with a radically modernist design that horrified supporters of "starved classicism." The design was never to be executed, and the radical modernists began to strike back with attacks on John Russell Pope's designs for the National Gallery of Art and the Jefferson Memorial. In the ensuing struggle between the two extremes, condemned so roundly by Frank Lloyd Wright in 1930, Art Deco got lost in the aesthetic shuffle. Only now are we beginning to retrieve it.

3
ART DECO—THE ARCHITECTURAL FORMULAS

An eclectic style, Art Deco drew freely on the International Style, the Vienna Secession, Aztec ornamentation, Cubism, and machine aesthetics. The first major quality of Art Deco was its effort to appear modern—or historically self-aware—through symbolism. Most of the preeminent symbols of the modern era appear on Washington's Art Deco buildings. Low-relief car, train, airplane, and ocean liner symbols are incorporated in Paul Cret's Calvert Street Bridge, renamed for Duke Ellington. In another design, Cret inserted sculptures of mechanical engineering on the main façade of the government's Central Heating and Refrigeration Plant: small representations of what was going on inside, and explicit symbols of the cult of the machine—pictorial symbols the International Style would have deemed "nonfunctional" and thus superfluous. The Federal Trade Commission building, otherwise bare of Deco, has remarkable cast-aluminum doors emblazoned with clipper planes and ocean liners.

The use and selection of materials played a crucial part in the stylistic development. New, inexpensive materials furthered the search for alternative forms. Cast-metal spandrels and terra-cotta panels replaced the load-bearing stone wall and limestone facing, thus facilitating the use of reinforced concrete frames and structural steel. New metal alloys, colored glass, and plastics contributed substantially to Deco's expression of elegance.

A second important principle of Art Deco was to convey a feeling of velocity and machine elegance. Both radical "purists" and Deco architects shared the fascination of machine aesthetics and explored the design implications of innovative engineering. Steel frame, reinforced concrete, and lightweight building materials supported the idea of modernity as means and ends. Still, the Deco architects went further in striving for a look of elegant smoothness. Sweeping lines in vertical or horizontal ribbon windows and corner turns through bay windows were hallmarks of mid-to-late 1930s Deco.

Before the streamlined Deco of the later period, the directional emphasis was verticality. Additional linework was created by projecting brick courses to exaggerate the verticality, which was further emphasised by opening the cornice line, with semicolumns and brick stripes projecting even further into the sky. This outcropping of the cornice line, one of the truly original devices in Deco architecture, found its ultimate expression in New York, where Deco is often equated with the Skyscraper Style. But even in Washington—with its height limitation imposed by the city's zoning regulations—the successful achievement of a sense of verticality remains impressive.

The archetypal design feature of Art Deco is the ziggurat. This basic motif was used so extensively that it served for a while as the trademark of the style. Its jagged rhythm was an ideal pattern to focus observers' attention. The ziggurat helped to terminate a

The ubiquitous ziggurat motif of Art Deco is featured here at 1727 R Street, NW, designed by William Barrington and completed in 1939. Decorative ceramic tiles were an added touch of flamboyance.

The ziggurat-crowned summit of the Cafritz Construction Company's Majestic apartments at 3200 16th Street, NW, designed by Alvin Aubinoe and Harry L. Edwards and completed in 1937.

column, advertised the building by an ascending roof line, and emphasized the entrance.

The third characteristic design principle was the ornamental treatment of the prominent parts of a building. There was no hesitation in juxtaposing traditional and modern materials. Before the 1920s, this would have been heresy. Aluminum with brick, stainless steel with marble, Formica with fruitwoods, all created sharp contrasts and made the new materials appear particularly elegant. The entrance to the apartment building on 2511 Q Street, NW, still looks as slick as the day it was built, with its shiny aluminum, glass brick, and Vitrolite, clad on the rough brick surface.

Not all parts of a building succumbed to Deco styling. Ornamental treatment was concentrated on the most *visible* parts of the structure: entrance, ground floor, corners and edges, cornice and roof line. A mundane reason for this had to do with the availability of decorative building components offered by terra-cotta and aluminum manufacturers. The most readily available prefabricated or custom-designed elements were doors, canopies, window spandrels, railings, fixtures, and assorted fittings.

Most Washington Deco buildings fall into the middle range between façades encrusted with Deco motifs and more austere ornamentation. Typical examples of a modest use of motifs are the garden apartments of the late 1930s: only the entrances are highlighted to reveal the decade of construction.

The birth of an architectural style is not an isolated phenomenon, a creative invention by designers independent of engineers, building suppliers, and technological developments. As the second half of the nineteenth century had its railway stations, exhibition halls, mechanized factories, and company housing, the years from 1920 to 1940 saw the spread of movie theaters, chain stores, and large-scale housing projects using mass-produced metal alloys, aluminum, cast stone, glass brick, and plastics. It was in these new categories of buildings that the new style was first and most consistently applied.

Washington's builders and architects, with the exception of the theater designers and the prefabricator John Joseph Earley, relied upon mass-produced aluminum and terracotta products to design stylish buildings. Building components of remarkable Art Deco design became available from regional and national manufacturers after the late 1920s. The use of such products in Washington buildings is confirmed by advertisements from professional journals.

Building components such as aluminum spandrels or lighting fixtures, which involved costly molding forms, were offered in a limited set of sizes and styles. Advertised in periodicals and in the comprehensive Sweet's Catalogue, they comprised a standard set ranging from Tudor, Georgian, and Federal to "Classic Modern" and "Modernistic."

Other products, notably terra cotta, marble, and limestone, remained custom-designed elements and gave the architect a considerable amount of freedom. This freedom rep-

Decorative aluminum spandrels grace the Kennedy-Warren apartment building at 3133 Connecticut Avenue, NW. The panels were produced by Alcoa Aluminum and advertised in architectural and construction journals as late as the forties.

A delicate Deco floral pattern on the Cafritz apartment at 2000 Connecticut Avenue, NW, illustrates the use of limestone and terracotta panels as well as the compact character of Deco floral motifs, which differed from the more sinuous patterns of Art Nouveau.

The striking, jazzy surfaces produced by glass brick and sandblasted Vitrolite are apparent in this entrance detail from Rock Creek Gardens West at 2511 Q Street, NW at the northern edge of Georgetown.

In 1935 the Vitrolite Company advertised its wares in *Fortune* magazine, claiming that the decorative glass product "attracts trade as nothing else can." The façade variations prove that the zigzag and streamline idioms represented related options for designers to use or combine throughout the 1930s.

resented a challenge which, as a general rule, was only taken up in the most prominent part of the building—the entrance.

When the architect or sculptor could not find a suitable form, he produced an accurate hard-line drawing or charcoal sketch, which was then translated by the manufacturer into a plaster model. After conferring with the architect, the definitive version was carved or molded in the final material.

The later decline of the prime Deco materials—terra cotta, cast stone, and ironwork—can be attributed to their individualistic application. Other products, the mass-produced and more standardized elements such as aluminum spandrels and industrial windows, made the easy transition into the post-Deco era of curtain-wall façades.

The building industry of the 1920s and 1930s experienced a fast-paced development. Research and development concentrated in three areas: white metal and aluminum, structural glass, and plastic products. New methods of fabrication and marketing introduced products with unprecedented properties of durability, strength, lightness, and convenience.

The most widely used metal was aluminum, with its outstanding qualities of light weight and malleability. Other white metal alloys favored were chrome-steel, chrome-nickel steel, and nickel silver, which appeared under a variety of trade names such as Allegheny, Enduro, Stainless, Nirosta, or simply Nickel Silver. Bakelite, the first commercially known synthetic resin, dates from 1909. By the mid-1930s all the important plastic products used today were on the market: Textolite, Resinox, Formica. Plastics were the epitome of modernity. They were *not* a modernized building material like glass or metal, but a completely new product, and were mostly used in stores, lobbies, movie theaters, bus stations, bars, dinettes, and similarly transient settings. Exceptions confirm this rule, especially when a compromise was employed. The tops of the reading tables in the Thomas Jefferson Building of the Library of Congress were made of Formica, according to the *Federal Architect*:

The wood effect was obtained by placing a layer of thin veneer walnut in the pile of lamination near the surface, so that when the pile was pressed together you had the beauty of wood combined with the resilient quality of the formaldehyde material. The architect's dream, seldom realized, has always been imperishable beauty.[1]

The utilization of glass underwent expansion into the field of structural glass, and the old technique of glass etching, widely used during the Art Nouveau epoch, was continued and revived by means of sandblasting. Two new major glass products, plate glass (in the version of Vitrolite) and glass block, introduced in this country around 1934, quickly gained in popularity and were widely used. Vitrolite and its variations (Carrara glass and Glastone) became a typical Deco material. Its polished surface on entrances and store fronts conveyed a modernistic look. Glass blocks were used in all types of structures, from warehouses to apartment buildings. Considering the hesitation to introduce new materials in the traditionally more conservative home-building sector, the wide acceptance of glass blocks is impressive.

The new building materials of the 1920s and 1930s—white metals, plastics, structural glass—have significant properties in common: they all have extremely hard, shimmering, sparkling surfaces. This quality concurred with Art Deco's search for elegance, and made the new materials equivalent to—or a good enough substitute for—more traditional building materials.

4
ART DECO COMES TO WASHINGTON

Unlike New York, where the rage for Art Deco was immediate, Washington was slower to adopt the style. The earliest, cautious attempts can be glimpsed in buildings like Horace Peaslee's The Moorings (1901–09 Q Street, NW), Louis Justement's Harvard Hall (1650 Harvard Street, NW), Harvey Warwick's Park Central (1900 F Street, NW), George Santmyers's Senate Courts (120 C Street, NE), Robert Beresford's Tower Building (1401 K Street, NW), and Ralph T. Walker's C & P Telephone Company building (730 12th Street, NW), all of which were built between 1927 and 1929. Aztec-looking Deco in its early phase was reflected in the Sedgwick Gardens apartments at 3726 Connecticut Avenue, NW, designed by Mihran Mesrobian, and the Kennedy-Warren Apartments at 3133 Connecticut Avenue, designed by Joseph Younger. Both buildings were built in 1932.

It was only with the New Deal's arrival that Deco burst forth as a Washington vogue. The major Washington Deco architects were Alvin Aubinoe and Harry L. Edwards, both of whom specialized in residential buildings for the Cafritz Construction Company; Robert O. Scholz, who produced a diversity of residential and commercial structures; Irwin Porter and Joseph Lockie, who produced commercial and institutional buildings in collaboration with John J. Earley's pioneering concrete prefabrication studio; Joseph Abel, whose work developed to a point mid-way between Deco and the International Style; and George T. Santmyers, whose specialty was Deco garden apartments, usually clustered into multiblock districts.

Deco design was also reflected in the work of out-of-town firms that designed for the larger Washington businesses: Abbott, Merkt & Company's designs for the Hecht Company and Woodward & Lothrop warehouses are probably the best examples. Others are the movie theaters designed by John J. Zink (of Baltimore) and John Eberson (of New York), along with Thomas Lamb's design for the Trans-Lux Theater. The architects of federal buildings, men such as Paul Cret, Milton Medary, and Edward Bennett, were architects of the "starved classical" school and they applied both the highly ornate and more streamlined features of Art Deco to their buildings, the former for use in interior design and the latter for exteriors. Most of these men were senior partners in out-of-town firms like Zantzinger, Borie and Medary, and Bennett, Parsons, and Frost. The architectural team of Douglas Ellington and Reginald D. Wadsworth had general charge of the design of Greenbelt, Maryland, and theirs is the work so beautifully reflected in the Greenbelt Center School. A number of well-known Washington architects like Louis Justement and Waldron Faulkner produced Deco buildings without adopting the style as a major theme in the course of their careers.

And finally—preeminently—there was John Joseph Earley, the wizard of prefabrication, whose "polychrome" process of concrete slab construction was a work of pioneering genius.

Washington's Art Deco is most conveniently classified by functional building categories. The attempt to group buildings by stylistic features fails because a Deco building frequently contains several elements from the whole form vocabulary. The presentation of Art Deco by building types permits us to follow the development as well as the different applications of the style. The distinction of Art Deco by building type was reinforced by a specialization among the architects and builders. This is most clearly visible in the work of John Eberson and John J. Zink, who specialized in movie theaters. Alvin Aubinoe left his imprint with several Deco apartment houses as well as with some elegant office buildings downtown. The most distinct specializations can be found in the work of George T. Santmyers, who usually worked with garden and mid-rise apartments, and John Joseph Earley, who built single-family houses composed of prefabricated mosaic concrete panels of outstanding craftsmanship. Earley also produced decorative precast panels for use by other architects. For the majority of builders and architects, Art Deco represented a repertoire of details to be used as long as the style lasted.

Each of the building categories exhibits stylistic differences. As a general rule, the commercial buildings incorporated Art Deco most readily. Stores and movie theaters were deliberately "modernistic." Similarly, apartment houses used Art Deco extensively to promote a glamorous image. At the other end of the scale, long-lasting institutional buildings—government buildings and churches, for example—reflected historical continuities in ways that were not quite flexible enough to incorporate Art Deco in its more flamboyant moods.

The following presentation of the Art Deco buildings in Washington is grouped according to the following categories: Residential, Commercial, Recreational, and Institutional.

Apartment Houses and Dormitories

By the 1930s, the ease of apartment living was having its effect upon Washington. Opulent apartment dwellings had already existed for several decades, and the latest apartments provided special services like catering, restaurants, stores, and even ballrooms. The three prime locations for apartments, besides the city center, were Massachusetts Avenue, Connecticut Avenue, and 16th Street, all in Northwest. Many of the 1930s apartment houses were traditionally designed; yet significant numbers of Deco-related apartments graced these commuting corridors.

The architecture of Massachusetts Avenue was largely traditional in style, except close to the city center, where some solidly Art Deco apartment houses were constructed, notably Robert O. Scholz's General Scott and Bay State apartments and Alvin Aubinoe's Winthrop House. The General Scott and the Bay State are probably the best residential work of Scholz (1896–1978), who moved to Washington from New Jersey in 1918 and started his own architectural firm in the early 1930s.

Connecticut Avenue, an elegant address for apartment living in the thirties, accepted the new style mainly as an additional decorative element on basically conservative buildings. Notable exceptions are the building at 4801 Connecticut Avenue, designed by David L. Stern and Joseph Abel in 1938 (its extraordinary flaring cantilever of aluminum over a circular glass-bricked foyer represents Deco at its most exuberant); 2929 Connecticut Avenue, designed by Joseph Abel in 1936; and 2000 Connecticut Avenue, a somewhat bulky but consistent Art Deco apartment house designed by Alvin

The Cafritz Company's Majestic apartment building, at 3200 16th Street, NW, represents a triumph of Washington Art Deco and a tribute to broader inspirations, particularly derived from New York. The towers of bay windows, for example, are reminiscent of New York's Rockefeller Apartments, designed by J. André Fouilhoux and Wallace K. Harrison. The name was perhaps inspired by New York's Majestic apartments designed by Irwin Chanin. (Courtesy Theodor Horydczak Collection, Library of Congress)

A. Aubinoe, who produced his masterworks on 16th Street. Two rather prominent apartment houses, the Kennedy-Warren and Sedgwick Gardens, incorporate a number of handsome but early and transitional Deco details: this is Deco in its primal phase.

Sixteenth Street, one of the city's major approaches and a central axis in the original L'Enfant plan, is architecturally one of the most interesting streets in Washington. For nearly three miles, it displays an outstanding variety of public buildings, churches, mansions, and apartment buildings. The unique architectural value inheres in the diversity of neo-Romanesque, classicist rigor, and flamboyant fin-de-siècle. In this sense, 16th Street has always represented an architectural challenge.

Two of the very finest Art Deco apartment houses in Washington were built on 16th Street, the Majestic (3200) and High Towers (1530), both designed by Alvin Aubinoe

The entranceway to the Majestic apartments was standard for Deco buildings designed by the Cafritz team of Alvin Aubinoe and Harry L. Edwards. The elements were almost certainly prefabricated, since identical entrances appear on New York apartment buildings along the Bronx's Grand Concourse.

The dramatic lines of the Cafritz apartment building High Towers are powerful enough to catch the eye while nonetheless blending with sedate Victorian neighbors along 16th Street, NW.

in partial collaboration with Harry L. Edwards. Both represent a harmonious blending of overall form with stylistic details. The synthesis is unpretentiously achieved by an interplay of bay windows, cornice lines broken by ziggurats, a succession of vertical lines, and handsome Deco entranceways, of aluminum, glass brick, and stone. These two outstanding buildings are of the same high standard of Art Deco architecture as Deco apartments in other cities (such as 1500 Grand Concourse in the Bronx).

Similar qualities can be found in the Park Crescent (2901 18th Street, NW), Ogden Gardens (1445 Ogden Street, NW), and Otis Gardens (1445 Otis Place, NW), all designed by Alvin Aubinoe and Harry L. Edwards. The Gwenwood (1020 19th Street, NW), designed by Edwards alone and demolished in 1981, displayed the same entranceway as the Majestic, High Towers, and the Park Crescent, but with a handsome and costly variation in materials. The aluminum doors were framed in glass mosaics of red and gold, which in turn were surrounded by black marble pilasters.

Aubinoe and Edwards formed a cohesive architectural team at Cafritz Construction Company until 1938, when Aubinoe formed his own construction company. Alvin L. Aubinoe (1903–1974) was born in Washington and attended the University of Maryland. After working for Cafritz as manager of construction from 1932 to 1938, he ventured forth on his own and became a very prominent Washington builder. His flamboyant summer residence at Rehoboth Beach was popularly known as the "pink palace."[1] At the height of his architectural career, Aubinoe handled the motifs and the idioms of Art Deco with an ease and consistency unparalleled by other local architects. Among the nonresidential buildings he designed or commissioned were the Wire Building (1000 Vermont Avenue, NW), designed in 1948, and the Commonwealth Building (1625 K Street, NW), designed by Harvey Warwick for Aubinoe's construction company in 1941.

Warwick (1893–1972), whose protean designs ranged from the earliest Deco-tending buildings in Washington (the Westchester Hotel) to Colonial Village in Arlington, Virginia, was a close business associate of developers Morris Cafritz and Gustave Ring. The Commonwealth Building reveals how his style, like that of so many Washington architects of this period, developed from the highly ornate and eclectic look of the late 1920s to a style rather neatly poised between Art Deco and the International Style by the early 1940s.[2]

Aubinoe's steady associate Harry L. Edwards (1902–1958) followed a similar path. A native of Florida, Edwards came to Washington to study architecture at George Washington University from 1920 to 1923. From an early collaboration on the Kennedy-Warren Apartments with Joseph Younger, Edwards went to work at Cafritz. Not only was his work reflected in buildings like the Gwenwood, and in his numerous architectural collaborations with Aubinoe—including, apparently, the Wire Building—but he also helped design the residence of Morris Cafritz on Foxhall Road and even played a role in designing the Pentagon.[3]

Several other prominent Washington architects contributed to the city's heritage of Deco or Deco-influenced residential buildings. Among the most ornate designs were those of Mihran Mesrobian (1889–1975), designer of several notable hotels including the Carlton (now the Sheraton-Carlton), the Hay-Adams, and the Wardman Park (later the Sheraton Park). Mesrobian, born in Turkey of Armenian parents, studied architecture in Istanbul and came to the United States after World War I.[4] The chief architect for developer Harry Wardman, Mesrobian designed the remarkable Sedgwick Gardens, among the most ornate and eclectic Deco structures in Washington, along with a number of later Deco apartments such as the Macklin (2911 Newark Street, NW) in 1939. His own residence at 7410 Connecticut Avenue in Chevy Chase, which he designed and built in 1941, shows that he too would eventually develop a modern adaptation of Art Deco and the International Style.

Joseph Abel's stunning lobby in the Governor Shepherd Apartments—named for Alexander Shepherd, the political "boss" of Washington during the Gilded Age—was combined with the overall functional lines of the building to win praise in architectural journals. (Courtesy Theodor Horydczak Collection, Library of Congress)

A more radical shift can be seen in the work of Joseph Abel (1905–), whose design for the Shoreham Hotel in 1930 blended Deco with Renaissance revival. Born and raised in Washington, Abel worked as an apprentice draftsman at the firm of George Santmyers during the 1920s, and later worked as a draftsman for Arthur Heaton. In the mid-1930s, following his success in designing the Shoreham, Abel founded the firm of Dillon and Abel with another apprentice of Santmyers, Charles Dillon. The firm was successively Dillon and Abel, Berla and Abel, and Abel and Weinstein. By the early 1940s, Abel's designs for Washington House (2120 16th Street, NW); the apartments in the 2700 block of Wisconsin Avenue, NW, particularly Highview (2700); the Croydon (1815 17th Street, NW); and the Governor Shepherd Apartments (2121 Virginia Avenue, NW) displayed an economy of line directly inspired by the International Style combined with unmistakable Deco flourishes. The Governor Shepherd Apartments, boasting an extremely elegant Deco lobby, were lauded in 1940 in the *Guide to Modern Architecture—Northeast States*, published by the Museum of Modern Art in New York. Especially worthy of note in the editor's view was the Governor Shepherd's "mechanical ventilation system," which provided a "complete air change for the entire building every 3 minutes."[5]

The buildings of Louis Justement (1892–1968) followed the same pattern, from the intricacies of Harvard Hall in 1928 to the spare lines of his Meridian Hill Hotel (2601 16th Street, NW) in 1942. But even in the 1940s, the work of such architects could suddenly revert to explicit Art Deco, as Justement's design for the 1946 Post Building (1012 20th Street, NW) amply proves.

Thus for many of the architects active in Washington, Art Deco represented a series of decorative elements to be combined with traditional and radical approaches, from Renaissance revival to classical to the International Style. Many of the Deco details thus applied had features in common, such as decorative entrances, jagged cornices, stream-lined fenestration, and buff-colored brick. Yet all of these features were frequently custom designed. No terra-cotta relief is the same, no cornice line is exactly alike, but all are variations of Art Deco motifs. Only where prefabricated, mass-produced elements were used did a standard vocabulary show; for example, the same Alcoa aluminum spandrel can be found in the luxury Kennedy-Warren apartment house as well as on a modest downtown storefront (516 12th Street, NW).

Cast-stone and terra-cotta moldings were the most adaptable elements and they can be found in almost all Deco buildings. Individually cast, they were used most extensively around entrances, as spandrels to accentuate the vertical ribbon windows, and for break-ing up the cornice line. The roof line is often a combination of ornamented lintels, capstones on vertical brick courses, and a jagged cornice line. Sometimes a third material is added to the brick and stone façades: enameled metal spandrels on Connecticut Gardens (1915 Kalorama Road, NW) and colored ceramic tiles on 1727 R Street, NW. The stonework garnishing the entire ground floor of many apartment houses around the turn of the century was reduced in the 1930s to a decorative use of limestone or terra cotta around the entrance. There are as many variations of this as there are Deco buildings.

In bas-relief ornamentation the entire range of Art Deco motifs can be found: floral forms, abstracted shells, and geometric zigzag. The small apartment house at 3150 16th Street, NW, incorporates its own address in the relief above the entrance door. Terra-cotta blocks were used as spandrels and lintels in Mesrobian's design for the Macklin.

The basic material for Washington's Deco apartment buildings is tan-colored brick, assuming the role of a backdrop for limestone or terra-cotta ornament. Only rarely is a tonal or textural variety shown through an interspersing of a colored brick course.

An exception is William Harris's design for the Park Tower (2440 16th Street, NW), an early Deco building of 1928 where the usual proportion of brick to terra cotta is completely reversed. Another exception is the early Senate Courts apartment house (now used for offices). Although the architectural concept is comparable to that of many later Deco buildings, the stonework combines Art Deco patterns with floral motifs in the undulating Art Nouveau manner, thus making of Senate Courts one of these rate examples of architectural transition, similar to the office building of the C & P Telephone Company.

An integral part of any swanky Deco apartment building is of course the *lobby*. There are times, in fact, when the image of a Deco apartment building derives more from its lobby than from anything else. Interestingly, some flamboyant Deco buildings have wholly unassuming lobbies—white stucco walls and plain aluminum elevator doors—while some otherwise undistinctive Deco buildings have sumptuous, extraordinary lobbies; the façade of the Delano, for instance (2745 29th Street, NW), designed by Santmyers in 1941, does little to reveal that it contains one of the very finest Deco lobbies in Wash-ington.

Two other outstanding Deco lobbies can be found in Santmyers's Normandie apartments (6817 Georgia Avenue, NW), built in 1938 and in Robert O. Scholz's Eddystone apart-ments (1301 Vermont Avenue, NW), built in 1937. Both of these little-known but prolific

Belying the notion that streamlining totally dominated 1930s design, the ornate side of Art Deco is alive in the lobby of the 1938 Normandie apartment-hotel designed by George T. Santmyers. The tiled fountain opposite the mailroom was a touch of whimsy. (Courtesy Herbert Striner)

Plant motifs on the ceiling of the Normandie apartments' lobby were probably prefabricated elements. The entire lobby, including the original lighting fixtures, constitutes a time capsule of 1930s ambience. The apartment hotel is directly across from the Walter Reed army installation on Georgia Avenue, NW, perhaps to cater to the needs of transient service families. (Courtesy Herbert Striner)

Ornate Deco plasterwork is featured in the lobby of Milton Hall, designed by Robert O. Scholz for use as an apartment building in the late thirties, but now used as a dormitory by George Washington University. One-bedroom apartments rented for $52.50 per month—a fairly substantial sum in 1940.

Washington architects employed a combination of zigzag and streamline elements throughout their buildings of the later 1930s, a fact that underscores once again the impossibility of cleanly severing "Art Deco" and "Art Moderne." The Normandie lobby is especially fine and well preserved with its original Deco fixtures. The ceilings and gallery are rich in intricate plaster moldings, and a decorative fountain of glazed tiles adorns the hallway. The lighting fixtures are among the most subtly beautiful remnants of Art Deco in the city: tenuous remnants of the overall design that deserve to remain in their original settings.

Yet another excellent lobby, replete with elaborate aluminum railings, may be found in Milton Hall (2222 I Street, NW), designed by Scholz in 1938. The building, together with its near twin, Munson Hall, and a third building placed back-to-back, The Everglades (2223 H Street, NW), which, interestingly, was designed by Joseph Abel a year later in a style deliberately contrived to harmonize with Scholz's work, is now being used as a dormitory by George Washington University. The lobby's Deco touches have been well maintained by the university, and even the mail boxes—usually one of the first fixtures to be replaced—still bear carved Deco details. Lobbies with original ornamentation of this sort are increasingly rare as a result of unsympathetic modernizations.

In partial contrast to the ornate qualities of lobbies, such as the Normandie's, were Deco entranceways of a strikingly streamlined nature on buildings that otherwise reflected a highly subdued Deco character. Such entranceways employed stainless steel and aluminum, polished marble, glass brick, and black glass (or Vitrolite). The most remarkable examples of sleek Deco entrances can be found at 1417 N Street, NW (originally built in 1930 but adapted to the more streamlined variant of Art Deco in 1938 by architect Frank Tomlinson) and in Rock Creek Gardens West (2511 Q Street, NW), designed by Joseph J. Maggenti in 1939. The wide entrance featured on the N Street building is an interplay of glass brick, aluminum, and black Vitrolite. The Vitrolite panels on either side of the door were sandblasted to obtain the effect of vertical stripes, and symmetrical lights are contained in aluminum frames of a sunray pattern. A smaller entrance with the same combination of colors and materials is found in Rock Creek Gardens West, where the name of the building is sandblasted into the Vitrolite transom bar above the door in classic Art Deco lettering.

The sleek facade of the N Street building is matched by an equally modernistic lobby using the newest manufactured materials: Formica wall panels with differently colored wood imitations, stainless steel trim, and linoleum floor coverings.

The lobby of 1417 N Street, NW, remains substantially unaltered—a rarity in Washington. The treatment of the formica paneling is unmistakably "thirties," as are the original *torchère* floor lamps.

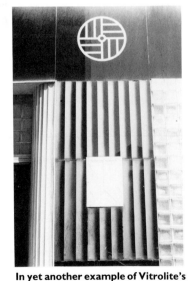

In yet another example of Vitrolite's commercial appeal in the 1930s, the building at 1417 N Street, NW, had a sleek façade added in 1938. The original entrance designed in 1930 was presumably more sedate.

A number of Washington's Art Deco apartment buildings from the later period were strongly affected by streamlining. While attempts to completely segregate zigzag "Art Deco" from streamline "Art Moderne" do not, as we have seen, succeed chronologically or stylistically—a point our discussion of the 1939 Library of Congress Annex will establish—a definite trend in the latter portion of the Deco era in Washington emphasized the streamline. No longer was verticality the dominating theme, for even taller buildings from the later 1930s and 1940s show attempts to balance verticality and horizontality, an equipoise revealed in the lines of Aubinoe's Winthrop House (1727 Massachusetts Avenue, NW) designed in 1940. Corners, instead of being sharp, vertical edges, were increasingly a matter of rounded bay windows. Vestigial traces of zigzag, however, were present in the spandrels between the ribbon windows in the angular placement of bricks, for example in the Bay State Apartments designed by Scholz in 1939 (1701 Massachusetts Avenue, NW).

Lobbies in several buildings designed by Scholz in the late 1930s show particularly fine use of the streamline idiom in long, sweeping lines and reflecting, polished surfaces. The lobby of Scholz's General Scott (1 Scott Circle, NW), completed in 1940, is composed of semicircular columns, rounded-off corners, and a large recessed circle for the indirect cove lighting so typical of many other Deco lobbies. The materials employed were costly: veneer marquetry wall panels, inlaid marble floor, and large wall mirrors.

Another streamlined lobby is in the Santmyers Deco apartment building at 2800 Woodley Road, NW, where free-standing vertical supports are treated as bundles of columns incorporating furniture—sofas and plant containers—and vertical strips of light. This is Santmyers's masterpiece. Through a pleasant coincidence, this apartment is located directly around the corner from the Delano, and the streamlined lobbies of the two buildings virtually rival one another for supremacy.

The suave appeal of the later streamlined Deco apartments cannot eclipse the charm of the earlier ornate structures. The two most celebrated early Deco apartment houses are the Sedgwick Gardens and the Kennedy-Warren, both on Connecticut Avenue. When it opened in 1932, the Kennedy-Warren was *the* smart address, named after its developers, E.S. Kennedy and Monroe Warren. The doorman still wears a uniform. The building represents one of the fullest expressions of "Aztec" Art Deco in the city. The granite facade to the side and above the main entrance is decorated with geometric animals in high relief interspersed with elements of Byzantine and Aztec patterns.[6] Pervasive terracing and the pyramid line of the roof above the entranceway are additional Aztec elements. The aluminum spandrels selected by the architect, Joseph Younger, are some of the finest prefabricated building components produced by Alcoa during the thirties. The most noteworthy Deco touch of the Kennedy-Warren is perhaps the impeccably preserved aluminum marquee, but Deco patterns pervade the structure from door fittings to exquisite elevator doors to the remarkable Deco ballroom, which features aluminum-panel reliefs showing Pan (or some anonymous satyr) with his pipes.

Even more ornate than the Kennedy-Warren is the entrance to the Sedgwick Gardens at 3726 Connecticut Avenue. The building's lobby is a potpourri of Romanesque and Byzantine, and its façade reveals Deco sunray motifs and bas-relief sculpture. But the crowning touch is the entranceway with its limestone friezes, its porte-cochère effect, and its remarkable opaque lamps. James Goode has described these lamps as "reminiscent of lighthouse beacons, perhaps to guide the residents back safely in their Packards and LaSalles. . . ."[7] The entranceway and the sculpture were designed by the building's architect, Mihran Mesrobian.

The other examples of Art Deco along Connecticut Avenue are far more sedate, with the exception of Stern and Abel's remarkable building at 4801 Connecticut with its extraordinary cantilever. The buildings designed by Aubinoe and Edwards on Connecticut

The imposing form of the luxury Kennedy-Warren apartment hotel towers over Connecticut Avenue, NW, near the National Zoo. The building was the ultimate in elegance in 1932, though the Great Depression canceled plans for a larger southern wing. The edifice remains a monument to a promising but tragically brief career: the architect, Joseph Younger, reputedly committed suicide. (Courtesy Theodor Horydczak Collection, Library of Congress)

In 1932 the lobby of the Kennedy-Warren reflected an eclectic mixture of traditional and modernistic elements. The marble facing on the columns and the decorative metal railings remain, though the rich walnut veneer has been partially lost, along with the elaborately painted ornamentation on the beamed ceiling. (Courtesy Theodor Horydczak Collection, Library of Congress)

The bright marquee of the Kennedy-Warren entrance remains unaltered, reflecting the popularity of aluminum during the thirties. One can easily visualize the sleek, sophisticated Packards and Auburns gliding up the driveway.

51

Sedgwick Gardens, the masterpiece of Turkish-born architect Mihran Mesrobian, combines a wealth of Byzantine ornamentation with Deco flourishes. The porte-cochère entranceway is a Connecticut Avenue landmark. (Courtesy Theodor Horydczak Collection, Library of Congress)

Avenue are not as distinguished as their work in the 16th Street corridor. Two other noteworthy buildings represent the eclectic work of Joseph Abel, the buildings at 2100 and 2929 Connecticut Avenue, the latter a blend of Art Deco, the International Style, and the influence of Frank Lloyd Wright. The lobby, with its rounded stucco columns, indirect lighting, and stainless-steel trim, is at par with any other Deco lobby in the city.

It was Abel's approach that foretold the evolution of Washington apartment buildings and provided a smooth transition from Art Deco to the styles of the postwar era. While enamored of Art Deco, Abel was also drawn to the ethic of the International Style with its "neue Sachlichkeit" of function: economical construction, hygienic environments, access to air and light, and the avoidance of "superfluous" ornament. These values, which Abel expounded in his book *Apartment Houses*, were increasingly accepted by fellow architects like Louis Justement in Washington.[8] A review of the apartments designed by Abel and Justement during the early 1940s provides a fitting, if highly tentative, answer to the question: when did Art Deco definitively end? The buildings of the early forties reveal that it just gradually—and almost imperceptibly—faded away.

This brilliant cantilevered marquee assures visitors that 4801 Connecticut Avenue, NW, is a smart address. The sweeping form was designed by modernist architect Joseph Abel in collaboration with David L. Stern. (Courtesy Herbert Striner)

The nautical influence in late-1930s design is already apparent in the sleek lobby of 2929 Connecticut Avenue, NW, designed by Joseph Abel and built in 1936. In contrast to the lobby's curvilinear forms, the building's exterior is rectilinear, displaying the influence of the International Style and the German Bauhaus.

The heavy growth in population in New Deal Washington produced a tremendous demand for housing. The answer was frequently found in the prototypical garden apartment. Nearly all of Washington's garden apartments were private developments, but most relied heavily on mortgage insurance from the newly created Federal Housing Administration (FHA). At the fringe of the denser city areas and spread throughout the adjoining suburbs, garden apartments proved to be extremely popular during the late 1930s and 1940s.

Building standards were set by the FHA, and distinctive architectural touches were centered on the entrances, cornices, and rooflines. The overwhelming majority of Washington's garden apartments were traditional English, Norman, or Colonial American structures. Arlington's Colonial Village (Gustave Ring, developer; Harvey Warwick, architect) and the Falkland Apartments in Silver Spring (Louis Justement, architect) set the standard.

Art Deco was reflected most vividly in *private* garden apartments. Its catchy, voguish appeal was very quickly apparent to the entrepreneurs who were contending for the lower-middle-class market. Public housing projects, on the other hand—sponsored by Washington's Alley Dwelling Authority or the planners of Greenbelt—related more closely to the International Style and its spartan ideals for worker housing.

The mystery man of garden apartment design in Washington is George T. Santmyers. This prolific designer of Deco garden apartments in the city was known as a "loner," who preferred to work for small, independent developers. Born in Front Royal, Virginia, in 1889, Santmyers was raised in Baltimore and opened an architectural firm in Washington in 1914, which he ran until his death in 1960.[9] Almost none of his papers have survived, and his colleagues, apparently, spurned him. Nonetheless, he left us the lobbies of the Normandie, the Delano, and 2800 Woodley Road, along with dozens of Deco garden apartments that were clustered into two coherent and explicit Deco districts. The architectural value of these goes beyond the individual buildings. As one reviewer, after visiting the "Deco District" in Miami Beach that was added to the National Register, responded to his own rhetorical question:

Are any of these buildings masterpieces? Probably not. Yet the Miami Beach Deco District in its entirety *is* a kind of architectural masterpiece, the work of virtually anonymous designers and architects, created quickly and largely by chance. It comprises an unparalleled streetscape [reflecting] a particular time, climate, and economy.[10]

So it is with the Deco garden apartment districts in Washington, D.C. The first of the two major districts is in Glover Park, between Georgetown and Wesley Heights. The two most distinguished Deco garden apartment complexes—both designed by Santmyers—were the Park View Terrace (Davis Place, 42d Street, and Edmunds Street, NW), completed in 1939, and Park Crest Gardens (W Street, 42d Street, and Benton Street, NW), completed in 1941. In both developments, all the entrances are subtle in design and harmonious in proportion. Tan brick with patterned spandrels, vertical strips of glass brick, and elegant marquees of aluminum are richly in evidence. In the same neighborhood are Deco garden apartments of red-brown brick, articulated with projecting or recessed brick courses and terra-cotta entrances.

The second Deco garden apartment district in Washington comprises the upper 14th Street corridor near Military Road, NW. On block after block, around 14th Street, Fort Stevens Drive, and Colorado Avenue, one can find a seemingly endless display of Santmyers' creativity. Bas-relief geometric patterns and floral motifs, an abundance of glass brick, and marquees of aluminum and Vitrolite create an impression that has to be experienced. A particularly remarkable form crowns the entrance to 1400 Somerset Place, NW (in this case the work of architect Bryan Connor): a concrete sculpture in

Typical of the decorative entrances to 1930s garden apartments in Washington, the entrance to 5746 Colorado Avenue, NW, designed by George T. Santmyers and built in 1938, proves that the taste for Deco embellishments persisted throughout the thirties. Of the dozens of garden apartments designed by the Santmyers firm, almost no two patterns of entrance ornamentation are precisely alike.

Park Crest Gardens, one of the two largest Deco garden-apartment complexes designed by the Santmyers firm in the neighborhood of Glover Park, was completed in 1941. The concrete panels at the entrance could possibly have been produced by the J.J. Earley studio, but neither Earley's nor Santmyers's records have survived to confirm this conjecture.

The Langston Dwellings project on Benning Road, NE, was the work of architect Hilyard Robinson, one of the few black architects in Washington during the thirties. Robinson, who also designed buildings for Howard University, studied in Europe and his work reflected the influence of Weimar Germany. The courtyard sculpture of blacks rising from slavery was executed by Daniel G. Olney. (Courtesy Theodor Horydczak Collection, Library of Congress)

Mount Dome, one of the few garden-apartment complexes to include stores, was constructed in the radial corridor of Pennsylvania Avenue, SE, in 1939. The abundant use of the zigzag forms is clearly in evidence at the building's main entrance.

the form of a gear pattern, a seemingly explicit tribute to the sort of machine aesthetics displayed in the Chicago World's Fair of 1933 and the New York fair of 1939. The best of the Santmyers buildings in the district is the Luzon (6323 Luzon Avenue, NW), built in 1938. Though many of the buildings are currently in poor condition, the potential for restoration and adaptive reuse is immense. Throughout the Washington suburbs are similar clusters: on Key Boulevard in Arlington, Virginia, and, in Maryland, in the Whittier Gardens adjacent to Takoma Park, in the Montgomery Arms in Silver Spring, and in Hyattsville's Prince George's Apartments, to name but a few.

One particularly notable cluster of garden apartments, the Lee Gardens in Arlington, constructed from 1941 to 1942 and designed by Mihran Mesrobian, represents a striking synthesis of Art Deco, especially in the use of glass bricks, and Colonial revival. While retaining traditional features like cupolas, yet constructing them of glass brick, the architect approached his task with delightful whimsy.

The most remarkable Deco garden apartment entrance in town is perhaps the Mount Dome at 3304 Pennsylvania Avenue, SE, designed by Bryan Connor in 1939. In this very late use of the ziggurat (in most cases ascending), the form is reversed: a descending cascade of zigzag patterns frames the door, and is continued on the wooden door itself.

A number of garden apartments in the late 1930s were built by public agencies. The primary concern, in the case of the Alley Dwelling Authority, was slum clearance and the provision of public housing. In the case of the Department of Agriculture's Resettlement Administration, the purpose of the Greenbelt cities was more complex, but nonetheless related. The requirements of low cost and standardization, along with more subtle intellectual trends, led mostly to the spartan lines of the International Style. The Langston Dwellings project, for instance (H and 21st streets, NE), designed in 1935–36 by architect Hilyard Robinson, one of the few black architects in Washington during the thirties, kept Art Deco motifs to an inconspicuous minimum, except for the beautiful Deco sculpture in the courtyard depicting blacks rising from slavery.

As garden apartments, the public units bear far more resemblance to German social housing projects of the late 1920s than to their local privately built counterparts.[11] Even the privately built Greenway Project (Minnesota Avenue, Ridge Road, and B Street, SE), designed by Harry L. Edwards of Cafritz in 1940, was similarly subdued. In the New Deal model town of Greenbelt, the severe lines of International Style housing are relieved with touches of glass brick in the usual Deco manner. The outstanding layout of Greenbelt, along with pleasant landscaping, prevented drabness. The housing units were offered with complete sets of custom-designed "Greenbelt furniture" in amber maple—furniture based upon contemporary Danish patterns. The furniture was available for credit purchase and the cost was usually little more than a few dollars a month.

Single-Family Houses

In 1935, when General Electric held a nationwide competition for the design of small houses, the reaction was unparalleled: more than 2,000 architects and designers submitted designs. The New American Home Competition was a badly needed stimulus, given the low productivity of the building industry during the Great Depression, combined with the tremendous need for housing.

The designs submitted were "functionalistic" and modern, with a few exceptions. The power of the International Style was particularly strong in the field of innovative housing, and the influence of Bauhaus design, the "maisons individuelles" of Le Corbusier, and the Prairie Style houses eclipsed the influence of Art Deco in this particular design sphere.[12]

Nonetheless, while residential building in Washington reflected this trend amid an overall pattern of traditional housing—especially Colonial revival—a number of "modernistic" Washington homes of the thirties and forties reflected both the International Style and significant traces of Art Deco. One of the very finest Deco-tending homes is the Cafritz Mansion at 2301 Foxhall Rd., NW, designed in 1936 by the Cafritz architectural team of Alvin Aubinoe and Harry Edwards. Though quiet and subdued, the design of the mansion incorporated many elegant Deco features in decorative trim and interior spaces. Another notable example is a Deco-cubist house in the somewhat unlikely setting of Camp Springs, Maryland. A clear-cut stucco box with sundecks, portholes, corner windows, and glass-block masonry, the building expresses a harmonious, differentiated composition.

An exact duplicate of the Camp Springs house, with the exception of its surface material—tan brick instead of stucco—can be found in the Lewisdale section of Hyattsville (6911 21st Avenue). Both of these houses were adapted from a catalogue design (no. 6692) published by the Garlinghouse Plan Service, a company centered in Topeka, Kansas, that advertised mail-order architectural plans. The founder of the company was Lewis Fayette Garlinghouse. Both of these Washington houses were built by their owners in the later 1940s.

A similar feeling can be found in the rectilinear but nautical-looking house at the corner of Calvert Street and Tunlaw Road, NW, designed by Dillon and Abel in 1938.

A very late variation on the 1930s streamline style is the beautiful Deco house at 2915 University Terrace, NW, designed by Howard D. Woodson in 1949. With corners rounded off and elongated horizontal lines stretching around the building, the house assumes a shiplike compactness on its sloping and wooded site. All details are still remarkably well preserved. Yet another noteworthy streamlined Deco house is improbably hidden away in Georgetown—at 3210 Reservoir Street, NW, surrounded by nineteenth-century row houses. The home was designed for Alexander Hawes in the late 1930s, and the architect was Theodore Dominick. Still other excellent examples of streamlined Deco houses can be seen at 1732 Portal Drive, NW, and 4012 25th Road in Arlington.

Besides these custom-designed single-family houses, an unsurpassed ensemble of semi-detached duplexes on upper 14th Street, NW—in the midst of the Santmyers Deco garden apartment district—provides clear evidence of Art Deco in residential building in Washington. At first glance, they appear to be traditional houses of a quasi-Jacobean character. But a closer examination shows a myriad of Deco and cubist features. Designed in 1935 by Harry Sternfeld, a professor of architecture at the University of Pennsylvania, the houses are replete with modernistic gateways, chimney stacks and porches, and interiors featuring maple paneling divided by aluminum trim. In their secluded setting, they typify the subtle delights of Deco in its understated versions, delights that await the viewer at many points around the city.

The Polychrome Houses

No survey of single-family Deco houses in Washington would be complete without a review of the "Polychrome Houses" designed by John Joseph Earley. For years, these unique houses have merited a special place in the history of Art Deco and in the history of Washington, D.C. They rank among the most outstanding prefabricated houses in the country, as much in their design as their superb craftsmanship.

John Joseph Earley (1881–1945) was the son of an Irish ecclesiastical stone carver, James Earley, who came to America in 1881 with his wife Mary. The family moved to

This prototypically "modernistic" house was built according to mail-order plans supplied by the Garlinghouse Plan Service of Topeka, Kansas. Stucco walls are the only major difference between this residence at 5516 Auth Road in Camp Springs, Maryland, and its near twin in Hyattsville, which is finished in tan brick.

Hidden away in a wealthy, secluded neighborhood west of American University, this extraordinary house was evidently built for a physician in the late 1940s. The winding, wooded road, University Terrace, is lined with an assortment of equally avant-garde residences from the fifties and sixties.

The second in the series of "polychrome houses" in Silver Spring featured large porthole windows. Earley hoped that the houses would alleviate the Great Depression's misery by providing low-cost housing of excellent craftsmanship for the common man.

The exquisite craftsmanship of John Joseph Earley is reflected throughout the concrete mosaic panels composing "Polychrome House #1" in Silver Spring. Even the wooden door contains inset panels of decorative concrete mosaic. (Courtesy Herbert Striner)

Even the chimneys of Earley's "polychrome houses" were merited worthy of decoration. This home, in a secluded middle-class neighborhood in southeast Washington, represents yet another Deco residence apparently built for a prosperous physician. Who knows how many other such houses are undiscovered? The Earley studio's records were largely destroyed by fire in the 1950s. This house is at 2911 W Street, SE.

Washington in 1890, where James Earley founded a studio devoted to sculpture and architectural stone carving. When his father died in 1906, John continued the Earley tradition with the help of Basil Taylor, a skilled workman in the studio.[13]

Blessed with extraordinary talent, Earley developed and substantially refined the medium of concrete mosaic. As Frederick W. Cron has explained:

Concrete . . . had a beauty of its own, hidden from view by the gray cement paste which stuck the aggregate particles together. Although the idea was not original with him, John Joseph Earley exposed the natural colors of these aggregate particles to view by removvng the cement paste from the surface. The result was a warm, attractive finish, the color of which could be varied from dazzling white through hundreds of color gradations to jet black. By applying superb craftsmanship to the scientific discoveries of their time, Earley and his associates perfected a process for producing exposed aggregate stucco. This led to the invention of a new art form—concrete mosaic—and . . . to the production of entire buildings by precasting concrete panels in a factory for later assembly.[14]

In the 1930s Earley's products gained nationwide attention and recognition. He was honored in his field by serving as president of its trade assocation, the American Concrete Institute, and through commissions in a number of cities. In Washington, numerous buildings were graced by one or more of his precast, multicolored concrete mosaics, all of which were formed by the staff of the Earley Studio in Rosslyn, Virginia. At least one architectural firm, Porter and Lockie, was a regular customer and used the precast panels supplied by Earley on most of its Deco-style buildings.

The polychrome houses were prompted by a social vision, the redoubtable Jeffersonian vision of independent freeholders, reworked in the Depression in "back-to-the-land" movements. Some of these visions were communalistic, like the one in the film *Our Daily Bread*, by King Vidor (1934). Others, like that of the theorist Ralph Borsodi, envisioned a retreat from profane cities to self-sufficient homesteads. Earley's vision was as follows:

The present social movement is a levelling one and it is entirely possible that we all will come to understand that the security which we desire for ourselves and our dependents lies in the nation's ability to provide food and shelter for everyone. It seems to me that the simplest way in which security can be achieved is to enable everyone to procure a small house and a plot of ground, which can be cultivated and which will produce sustenance.[15]

The medium he chose to employ, prefabricated concrete mosaic panels, offered a possibility "the like of which has never been known before, and the limits of which are the limits of human ingenuity", Earley declared.[16]

In 1934 Earley and his partner, Basil Taylor, started work on their first prefabricated small house. "Polychrome House Number One" was erected at 9900 Colesville Road in Silver Spring. It was quickly followed by a second one-story house next door in 1935, and by three two-story houses around the corner the same year. Polychrome House Number One was designed by architect J. R. Kennedy to Earley's specifications. Its prefabricated concrete wall panels were anchored on small structural concrete columns cast in place at each joint. The wall panels themselves were concrete mosaic in a multicolored form from which the term "polychrome" was derived. The main color—granite pink—was obtained using aggregates of red jasperite (a form of quartz). Other colors were derived from crushed natural stones and various ceramics and vitreous enamels. The brilliant and exquisite colors have lasted for fifty years with no apparent signs of fading. The precise nature of the polychrome process is a secret that apparently died with Earley.

A polychrome cornice and mosaic frieze surrounds Polychrome House Number One below the roofline. Buff-colored quartz was the material used in the fluted columns flanking the door, in the window trims, and in the corner pilasters. These finely crafted elements reflected a number of Art Deco motifs, particularly zigzag forms.

A Model "A" Ford truck assists in the construction of Earley's second polychrome house in 1935. This photograph appeared in December of that year in *Architectural Forum*. Earley's methods of prefabrication received nationwide attention and acclaim.

In the second polychrome house on Colesville Road, Earley made less extensive use of color. Instead, relief patterns—both recessed and raised—were applied, along with a new use of porthole windows, whose frames were embedded in the panels before casting.

A very similar house was built in a secluded neighborhood in Southeast Washington. Color mosaics were placed on various surfaces, and three insets of red and black mosaic concrete were inserted in the wooden door. The adaptability of concrete prefabrication is illustrated here in the lower-level garage that was constructed on the front yard's sloping land. This particular polychrome dwelling at 2911 W Street, SE, is perhaps the most beautiful house that the Earley studio designed. But the Silver Spring houses, including the three two-story houses on Sutherland Road, give a sense of what a neighborhood designed by the Earley methods might have become.

Such a neighborhood was never to be, for despite the remarkable houses built by Earley, the method of prefabricating concrete houses was never destined for mass production. Though more than 100 companies were offering prefabricated houses by 1935, including such potent distributors as Sears Roebuck, the national market was never significant. It remains to be seen whether Earley's exceptional achievement amounts to a mere curiosity or something of a dormant prophecy.

Office Buildings

From the late 1920s through the mid-1930s, the preponderance of Washington's office buildings were traditionally designed. While the Chrysler Building and the Empire State Building were flaunting the spirit of Art Deco in New York City, Washington's office buildings were Gothic, classical, and Renaissance revival.[17] The reasons for this can be traced to the conservative patterns set by the offices designed for the federal government as well as to a general slump in demand for private office buildings. When the government began to move into the newly completed buildings of Federal Triangle, it relinquished office space in dozens of private buildings it had previously leased, thus creating an overall glut on the office market.

Among the few office buildings designed in the Deco style before the late thirties, the building designed for Chesapeake and Potomac Telephone Company in 1928 by Ralph T. Walker is probably the finest. Walker's firm, Voorhees, Gmelin & Walker, was based in New York and designed almost all of the important company buildings for the Bell

Ralph T. Walker, designer of the first Deco skyscraper in New York, designed this building for the Chesapeake and Potomac Telephone Company in 1928. The building, at 730 12th Street, NW, features intricate floral "seed catalog" decoration, of a quality approaching Art Nouveau, within terraced borders of early Art Deco design. Such examples of stylistic transition are extremely significant.

Systems of New Jersey and New York. The Barclay-Vesey Building in New York City, completed by Voorhees, Gmelin & Walker in 1925, is one of the earliest Art Deco structures in America, having been completed the same year as the Paris exposition. It was featured by Le Corbusier in an early edition of his book *Towards a New Architecture*, and the editor of *American Architect* considered it the finest modern office building in America in 1925.[18] Walker was the principal architect. A graduate of MIT, he was honored by the American Institute of Architects, which awarded him its Centennial Medal in 1957.[19]

The C & P Telephone Company Building (730 12th Street, NW) is a masterfully subtle creation. The intricate ornamentation on the facade is a pattern of sinuous floral forms within terraced borders. This ornamentation is applied around the first three stories and repeated at the top story with a buff-brick interstice of three stories in between. Above the top story is a gable with an eagle in high relief at its axis.

The main lobby of the building is plain, but the vestibule is of exquisite proportions, decorated with green marble panels, a fine filigreelike grillwork, and a sunray-pattern ceiling with zigzag outline.

There is one other fact about the C & P Telephone Company Building: it records a remarkable transition, since its weaving floral patterns are a very late expression of Art Nouveau and its zigzag borders for the ornamentation are early Art Deco. Because examples of integrated architectural transition are rare, this fact alone makes such a building historically significant.

Another early Deco office building is the Tower Building (1401 K Street, NW), designed by Robert Beresford in 1928. The explicit Aztec pyramid atop this building compares with similar structures in New York City and elsewhere. The lobby has exceptional brass ornamentation and a very beautifully patterned marble floor.

Following a long hiatus during the early- to mid-1930s, office construction resumed in the late thirties and early forties. The Walker Building, sandwiched between much wider structures at 734 15th Street, NW, is rather easily overlooked. Yet the building, designed by Porter & Lockie in 1937, features some worthwhile Deco details, especially in its entrance and lobby. The door and window heads above ground level carry beautiful polychrome concrete panels by John Joseph Earley. Above the doorway, the concrete mosaic is echoed in an equally symmetrical aluminum grille with profuse shapes and lines. The second-floor windows are trimmed with fluted columns and horizontal mosaic stripes for the sill and lintel.

The quiet lobby, done in polished marble and reflecting mirrors, has fine examples of engraved and sandblasted elevator doors with dense Deco patterns, a noteworthy eagle-emblazoned mailbox, and an exquisite Deco chandelier.

Regrettably, a very fine low-level Deco office constructed at 1627 K Street, NW, in 1936—the Heurich Building, designed by Frank Russell White—was demolished in the 1970s.

Other Washington office buildings of the late thirties and forties were either composites of Deco and the International Style or out-and-out expressions of radical modernist functionalism. The Commonwealth Building (1625 K Street, NW), designed in 1941 by Harvey Warwick for Alvin Aubinoe's firm, has an interestingly proportioned façade and an outstanding lobby. Its shining terrazzo floor, inlaid with black and red bands forming rectangles, the richly tectured polished marble of its walls, and the black ceramic tiles of its ceiling are excellent enough, but the lovely undulation on the upper part of its walls makes for sweeping brilliance. The Commonwealth Building today has lost none of its modern appeal and remains among the most elegant office structures in the city.

The later Wire Building (1000 Vermont Avenue, NW), designed by Aubinoe's firm in 1948, is entirely stripped of ornamentation. Yet this McPherson Square building is

Sumptuous marble and delicate metal grillwork grace the vestibule of Walker's C & P Telephone Company building, one of the earliest expressions of Art Deco in the Nation's Capital, and one of the finest surviving Deco office buildings in the city.

66

Exquisite polychrome panels supplied by the Earley studio decorate the entrance to Porter and Lockie's Walker Building in the 15th Street financial district close to the White House. The firm of Porter and Lockie was a regular customer for Earley's products.

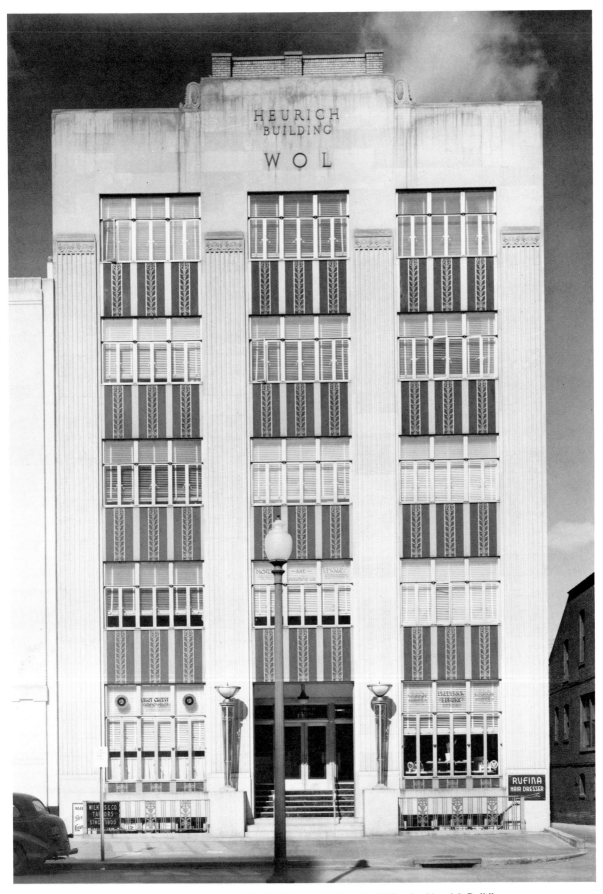

HEURICH
BUILDING

WOL

One of the rare Deco office buildings constructed in Washington during the 1930s, the Heurich Building on K Street, NW, was demolished in the early 1970s. A few doors away, the Commonwealth Building— fortunately much larger—still survives. (Courtesy Theodor Horydczak Collection, Library of Congress)

far too much an expression of the streamline style's exuberance to merit the term "functionalist." Featuring long, horizontal ribbon windows and a lintel of polished marble on the ground floor, it recalls one of the keynote buildings of modern architecture, the Schocken department store in Berlin-Chemnitz, designed by Erich Mendelsohn in 1930. Yet the Wire Building's streamline-style application remains peculiarly American.

If there is one building of the period that clearly merits the appellation "International Style" it is the Longfellow Building by William Lescaze (1741 Rhode Island Avenue, NW), completed in 1940. The famous Swiss-born architect designed the building in the spirit of the International Style at its most uncompromising. It was a herald of 1950s and 1960s design.

Shops, Stores, and Restaurants

Commercial Deco abounds in the Washington area. It represents Deco in its jazziest form, the voguish style from the age when "Swing was the thing." Its design vocabulary seemed to go with the music of Harry Warren and Al Dubin. Neon signs and Vitrolite façades were a visual counterpart of the "Lullaby of Broadway" and "Forty Second Street." And yet the smartness of the style was doomed, in the manner of everything trendy, to fall before newer and successive waves of fashion in the 1950s and 1960s.

The familiar progression from ornate to more streamlined Art Deco can be seen in the Sears Roebuck stores. These larger commercial structures were designed by out-of-town firms. The store at 911 Bladensburg Road, NE, was designed by Nimmons, Carr and Wright in 1929 with the usual Aztec touches. Its richly decorative façade is an interplay of terra-cotta reliefs and bricks. Its antithesis, at 4500 Wisconsin Avenue, near Tenley Circle, was designed by John Stokes Redden of the Sears property department in 1940. Of low profile, the building is perfectly adapted to the irregular site. Great care was taken in the selection of an exterior texture for the architectural concrete walls: after various sample sections of walls were cast, the architects chose panels made with circular-sawed boards to achieve the desired natural roughness. The single panels were joined by rustications formed by V-cut strips, thus concealing both construction and control joints and obtaining richly articulated concrete walls. The plasticity and texture of this beautiful composition and the continuity of its expressive horizontal and vertical linework are reminiscent of the later designs of Frank Lloyd Wright.

Another distinguished commercial building by an out-of-town firm is the former Remington Rand Building at F and 13th streets, NW. Designed by the famous Chicago architectural firm of Holabird and Root, this 1935 structure is a boxlike design with soft edges and finely detailed windows. A sculptured "glasshouse" quality is present across the façade. While perhaps not the finest creation of Holabird and Root, the Remington Rand Building ranks among the most modernistic and streamlined buildings on F Street. In its early days, the Remington Rand Building housed the streamlined Mayfair Restaurant—"The Cafe of All Nations"—featuring murals by the studio of Joseph Urban.

Out-of-town architects designed almost all of Washington's five-and-dime stores. A number of these classic American structures survive in good condition, though interiors have sadly but inevitably been altered. Despite the "standardized" architectural quality of chain store design, the Washington creations of Kresge's and Woolworth's retain some significant features of individuality. The Kresge's at 434 7th Street, NW, retains some very good Deco trim and appropriate lettering on its windows. The Woolworth stores display fascinating terra-cotta parapets featuring the signature touch of the continuous red band with gold letters. The Georgetown store at 3111 M Street, NW (recently sold), has a particularly streamlined parapet.

Though frequently taken for granted, the Sears Roebuck department store above Tenley Circle on Wisconsin Avenue, NW, is quite remarkable. Brilliantly adapted to its site, the building designed by John Stokes Redden in 1940 was the state-of-the-art in concrete construction with abundant graceful details of streamlining in an asymmetrical format.

The chain store formula was copied by a number of local businesses. Especially worthy were the stores produced by the Washington firm of Hahn's Shoes. These extremely elegant smaller structures were "high '30s" design: one can almost visualize Ginger Rogers stepping out of Hahn's in some crisp thirties outfit with spectator shoes—brown and white—a calf-length dress, and a nifty, rakish hat. The Deco appeal of these stores has been allowed to fall into decline and a number of them have been sold to other businesses—fireworks sales and the like. The Clarendon store, on Wilson Boulevard in Arlington, Virginia, was, until recently, among the best preserved, still carrying the original aluminum lettering.

Commercial Deco structures featured the usual building materials: terra cotta combined with aluminum trim, buff-colored brick, or concrete. Individual structures are found throughout the city and suburbs. Representative buildings were the Brownley's Building, designed by Porter and Lockie in 1932 (demolished in 1981), which used to contain the Blue Mirror Grill, yet another Deco-denizen of F Street; the Farmers Banking and Trust Company in Rockville, Maryland (4 Courthouse Square), designed by the Tilghman-Moyer Company in 1930; the Atlantic Electric Supply Corporation building at 3726 10th Street, NE, designed by William E. St. Cyr Barrington in 1938; the very streamlined Lansburgh's store at 418 7th Street, NW, designed by Porter and Lockie in 1940; the enormous Neisner Brothers department store at 1112 G Street, NW (demolished in 1981); "Aero Chevrolet" at 1101 King Street in Alexandria (demolished 1983); and dozens of small commercial structures along the Wilson Boulevard, Lee Highway, and Mount Vernon Avenue corridors in suburban Virginia.

The commonest application of commercial Deco, however, was in semidetached or contiguous storefronts stretched across a whole block. Early examples of this were the red brick/terra-cotta stores in the 7900 block of Georgia Avenue in Silver Spring and the similar structures in the heart of Takoma Park. Concrete or terra-cotta façades were applied to innumerable blocks of stores in the late 1930s. Many of these were adjacent to movie palaces: the stores built into the Penn Theater on Capitol Hill are an example

The Brownley's confection company commissioned Porter and Lockie to design two complementary buildings in the 1300 block of F Street, NW, in 1932. The Brownley's Building at 1300 F Street, the home of the Blue Mirror Grill, was ignominiously swept away by the Pennsylvania Avenue Development Corporation in the early 1980s. Surviving is 1309 F Street (above), though the first-floor level has been covered with a newer entrance. (Courtesy Theodor Horydczak Collection, Library of Congress)

of this, and the extensive one-story building around the Uptown Theater on Connecticut Avenue, with its unbroken display of commercial Art Deco, is among the best examples in the city. The streamline style, with its horizontality, is used to connect the shops in a continuous band from the Uptown Theater to the base of Mesrobian's Macklin Apartments, with which the stores intersect. On the other side of Connecticut Avenue, the pattern continues in structures like the Roma Restaurant. Some very beautiful aluminum spandrels, reminiscent of the Chanin Building in New York, were recently uncovered on the Roma's façade.

It was a small step from these commercial blocks to the shopping center of the late 1930s. From indoor shopping arcades (like the Chevy Chase Arcade in the 5500 block of Connecticut Avenue, NW) developers leaned toward centers that could easily accommodate automobiles; the neighborhood shopping centers adjacent to the Sheridan Theater (Georgia Avenue and Sheridan Street, NW), the Flower Theater in Takoma Park, and the center in the 4400 block of Connecticut Avenue, NW, which originally featured a bowling alley, are good examples. Another is the highly streamlined shopping center in the 3700 block of 10th Street, NE, designed by Hyman Cunin in 1938. Very rapidly, Deco shopping centers began to appear in the nearby suburbs: Arlandria Center (3800 block of Mount Vernon Avenue, Alexandria); Westover Center (5800 block of Washington Boulevard in Arlington); the Wheaton Shopping Center (11400 block of Georgia Avenue), whose neon signs are still remarkably well preserved; and the Queen's Chapel Center at the intersection of Queen's Chapel Road and Hamilton Street in Hyattsville. But the best of the Deco shopping centers is the heart of an entire Deco commercial district in Silver Spring. This shopping center at the intersection of Georgia Avenue and Colesville Road is a minor masterpiece of Deco streamlined forms, with its tan brick horizontally pinstriped in darker tones. Sweeping very gracefully around the corner to the nautical-looking Silver Theater on Colesville Road, the shopping center, designed by the firm of John Eberson in 1938, is also the focal point for a Deco district comprising several square blocks and including the Tastee Diner on Georgia Avenue, the streamlined Hecht's department store on Fenton Street and Ellsworth Drive, the Hahn's and J.C. Penney's on Colesville Road, and a cluster of Santmyers Deco garden apartments. Critic Benjamin Forgey recently assessed the value of the district as follows:

In a curious fashion, this cluster of buildings looks better than ever today. . . . There's nothing all that flashy about these buildings, now four decades old, nor anything all that ambitious. But there is color in panels of glass and tile, in striped brickwork, in once-shiny aluminum signs and trim. There is a modest, late-Deco decor in the fluted pilasters and rounded corners, and a sense of civility.[20]

When shopping centers were too ambitious, developers frequently applied Deco to existing commercial buildings. A well-known axiom of merchandising stresses a constant updating of "image." This principle was particularly rife in the years of the Depression, when the attraction of customers was a matter of survival. The step forward as a way out of the tumbling affairs was seen in the remodeling and modernization of the old premises. Consequently, "Modernize Main Street" became a 1930s catch-phrase of business.[21] The building industry sponsored campaigns like the "Modernize Main Street Competition" held by the Libbey-Owens-Ford Glass Company in 1935, the traveling exhibition of modern store fronts sponsored by the Pittsburgh Plate Glass Company in 1936, and the Pittsburgh Glass Institute competition of 1937.[22] And in 1935 the FHA was empowered to extend its loan insurance for commercial remodeling.[23]

The result of the modernization that swept through the shop-lined streets in the 1930s was both devastating and creative. Thousands of Victorian details disappeared behind aluminized brick, Vitrolite, or terra cotta. In many cases this left us with a legacy of beautiful Art Deco. In retrospect, it seems ironic that the threatened Deco façades of

This lavishly-executed Deco aluminum panel was recently uncovered on the Roma Restaurant's façade. The panel, however, which dates to 1936, has been ironically covered in part by a sign and an awning that obscure much of its beauty.

71

This Deco goddess, reveling in her possession of a prize peacock, illustrates the versatility of terra-cotta façade ornamentation. The façade, at 1211 F Street, NW, was applied by Wilbur-Rogers, Inc., a retailing firm, in 1931.

Whitlow's Restaurant, a humble establishment at 501 11th Street, NW, is a case study in Vitrolite façades applied to earlier buildings. Vernacular though it is, there is every reason to think about preserving this streamlined design. The year of construction and the designer remain unknown.

today were the result of the same commercial imperatives that earlier destroyed the Victorian designs.

The most widely used remodeling material was terra cotta, frequently combined with cast-aluminum friezes and spandrels. F Street had the most sweepingly Deco blocks in the city as a result of 1930s remodeling. Surviving treasures include a superb terra-cotta relief of a woman holding that favorite Art Nouveau and Art Deco denizen: a peacock.

Nearby, a commercial three-story structure at 512 10th Street, NW (originally a power company substation designed by John Loehler for PEPCO), is entirely covered with enamelled metal sheets. The beige and blue panels were fitted together like a puzzle with wrap-around edges and corners, added up to a fine, streamlined façade.

The simplest and quickest way to modernize a building was by the installation of a neon sign, and among the best examples is Arbaugh's restaurant on Connecticut Avenue, NW. Other noteworthy Deco restaurant façades can be seen at Whitlow's Restaurant (501 11th Street, NW), a very beautiful example of the Vitrolite façade; the Seven Seas Chinese Restaurant at 5915 Georgia Avenue, NW; the China Doll at 627 H Street, NW, with a stunning black Vitrolite façade, and Crisfield's Restaurant at 8012 Georgia Avenue, in Silver Spring. Among Deco delights in restaurant interiors, there is the Imperial Cafe at 613 Pennsylvania Avenue, SE, which has since been turned into a Deco-revival pizza parlor called "Machiavelli's." And among the most playful Deco touches on commercial structures are the entrance to Barrelhouse Liquor at 1341 14th Street, NW, and the unbelievable glazed-brick sign at the back of Progressive Cleaners at 4001 Lee Highway in Arlington (now temporarily obscured by a newer sign)—the black and white brick forms the pattern of the 1939 World's Fair Trylon and Perisphere. The lettering reads, in an almost Rooseveltian cadence, "Arlington is Progressive: So Are We!"

Standardized and Prefabricated Commercial Structures

Chain store and gas station architecture has a life of its own: the same models can be found across the country, regardless of local site conditions. Yet, surprising elements

"Arlington Is Progressive!" But progress is a relative concept, and the glazed-brick mural on the back wall of Progressive Cleaners in Arlington, Virginia, was recently painted over and covered with a plastic sign. The 1939 World's Fair Trylon and Perisphere are still the symbols of the firm.

of individuality await the connoisseur, as the writings of the American Society for Commercial Archaeology attest. In Washington a number of fine architectural examples of corporate design remain to be discovered.

Diners, in particular, have recently become the subject of photorealist art and nostalgic veneration. The most noteworthy Washington diners among the unremodeled specimens are the Tastee Diners in Silver Spring and Fairfax. The Silver Spring Tastee Diner is a splendid representation of vernacular design and streamline aesthetics: sweeping lines, rounded corners, wrap-around turquoise trim on a cream-colored background, and awnings that merge into the ventilating cupola overhead. Although the Tastee Diner was assembled in 1946, it represents the aesthetics of the 1930s unaltered in any way. From the onset of the diner craze in the late twenties, when hard-edged Pullman cars and trolleys were adapted to use as restaurants, diners evolved into the sleek confections of porcelain enamel, stainless steel, and glass block that would dazzle roadside America throughout the thirties and forties. The Silver Spring Tastee is a perfect representative of this machine-expressive style. So are the silver Tastee Diners on Lee Highway in Fairfax, Virginia, and in Laurel, Maryland. The Tastee Diner in Bethesda, Maryland, has been severely altered, alas.

Diners could be adapted to almost any empty site. The problem of meeting the requirement for larger dining areas beyond the standard size of diner production was solved by "split construction." The Silver Spring Tastee Diner was built and transported in two sections and assembled on location.

There were other short-order restaurants along the busy highways and shopping thoroughfares of Washington during the age of Art Deco, and two very enterprising chains of hamburger shops did battle with the diners for a share of the fast-food market: the White Towers and the Little Taverns. Both used design as an integral component of marketing.

One of the first of the East Coast hamburger chains, the White Towers had at least six stores in Washington. The only White Tower remaining today, at the corner of H and 13th Streets, NW, displays the typical shiny white surfaces, large expanses of glass, a tower on the corner entrance, and a row of gooseneck lamps along the roofline. The

A brand-new White Tower lunchroom, circa 1940, draws night-owl patrons at 14th Street, NW. (Photo by David Myers, courtesy Office of War Information Collection, Library of Congress)

image of the White Tower was that of a dependable and clean establishment. Numerous Art Deco details that were common on the earlier shops were stripped from the H Street store. The best example of the White Tower design was the streamlined restaurant built in Silver Spring (now destroyed).

The Little Tavern hamburger shops were distributed by the dozens throughout the city and suburbs and as far as Baltimore. They were neon-illuminated cottages, sheathed in white-and-green enamel. Their pitched roofs and dormer windows lessen their identity as Art Deco, but, as Lynne Heneson and Larry Kanter have said:

The Little Tavern is avant garde, featuring the bold design elements of the modern age—streamlining, neon, new materials in innovative ways. The effect is striking, demonstrating Little Tavern's timeless appeal. The combination of traditional form with modern materials and design images makes Little Taverns an important example of Art Deco. Even more, Little Taverns are a legend, not only as vernacular architecture, but also for their meaning to all who knew them, from corporate magnate to grill man to solitary midnight patron. . . . Seizing the characteristic Art Deco ideal of speed and simplicity best shown in airplane design, the architects of these buildings slowly eliminated decoration and detail, until what was left was a streamlined emblem. The store became a billboard and the motorist read the message quickly. Cleanliness, efficiency, convenience, homeyness—all of these were conveyed at a glance.[24]

The founder of the Little Tavern shops, Harry Duncan, built his first hamburger stand in Washington in 1927, and the chain expanded rapidly throughout the 1930s. The defining architectural Little Tavern approach was the use of the porcelain enamel steel panels both within and outside the structure. Charles E. Brooks and George E. Stone of the Stonebrook Corporation were responsible for the overall design, and Duncan applied it throughout his chain.

The most ubiquitous form of prefabricated commercial Deco design could be found in gasoline stations. Yet commercial remodeling imperatives have destroyed almost all of the more elaborate stations of the twenties and thirties in the Washington area. A notable exception is Bonfield's Texaco (6124 McArthur Boulevard, Bon Air Heights, Maryland), which was adapted from a house. The typical Deco gasoline station of the early 1930s

This 1940s advertisement for Little Taverns shows the firm at the height of its appeal. A thoroughgoing restoration and revival of the Little Tavern Shops has proceeded under the supervision of architect Tim Crosby. (Courtesy Gerald Wedren and Little Tavern Shops, Inc.)

A winsome waitress beckons to customers of Little Tavern Hamburger Shops in this circa-1930 advertisement. The crenelated, castlelike format of the architecture soon gave way to the still-familiar enameled, neon-clad, mock-Tudor cottage. (Courtesy Gerald Wedren and Little Tavern Shops, Inc.)

A masterpiece of streamlined design, the warehouse designed for the Hecht Company at 1401 New York Avenue, NE, was the work of the New York architectural and engineering firm of Abbott, Merkt and Company. The building was completed in 1937.

featured construction of terra cotta, where the range of ornate Deco details could be displayed in profusion.

Later, as the streamline aesthetic took over, the corporate designers of gas stations turned more and more to the stripped designs that Daniel Vieyra has called "functional."[25] Many prominent architects and designers submitted plans for model gas stations to the major oil companies, frequently under the stimulus supplied by the companies themselves in the form of contests.[26] Very few of the resulting prototypes, however, went into production. A major exception was Walter Dorwin Teague's design for a Texaco station that was replicated across the country in the thirties and forties. Other companies leaned heavily on Teague's design, especially the Austin Company in Cleveland.

A few of these functionalistic stations survive around the Washington area. Whether designed by Teague or some anonymous corporate architect, they share the same characteristics of cubistic form and clean-cut openings, shining white porcelain enamel steel panels intersected with colored trim and abbreviated canopies. Most examples of this building type are a happy, unassuming combination of the International Style and streamlined Art Deco.

Industrial and Transportation Buildings

Washington's Art Deco achieved its purest expression in the field of industrial design. One building—a palace of Art Deco at its most exuberant—deserves a nationwide reputation as a Deco masterpiece. It is the Hecht Company warehouse on New York Avenue, a wonder house of glass brick. Not a line is wasted in this obviously functional building, yet the form is expressive. Long ribbon windows of glass brick, with alternate bands of buff-colored brick, wrap around the building with a generous abstract pattern of black and white tile at the ground level. The dramatic effect of the building's northwest corner is similar to that of the May Company department store in the Miracle Mile of Los Angeles: the sweeping sides tuck in at the corner where a towering column of glass is topped with a crown.

Designed by the New York architectural and engineering firm of Abbott, Merkt and Company, the Hecht building was completed in 1937. It won a prize that year in a nationwide competition held by the Pittsburgh Glass Institute, and was lauded in *Architectural Forum* as "another vigorous demonstration of the potentialities of glass block which functions as wall and window. . . ."[27] At the building's dedication, Sen. Millard Tydings of Maryland praised its design as a monument to the "business genius which has made America the country it is," and the *Washington Herald* declared that it epitomized an "architecture that is destined to precipitate a revolutionary transformation in the appearance and utility of buildings in this country."[28] If there is any Deco building in Washington deserving unstinting praise—and preservation at any cost—it is this one.

The use of glass brick was a virtual craze that began in the mid-1930s and continued into the 1950s. Another remarkable example of its use in industrial Deco buildings is the Manhattan Laundry at 1326 Florida Avenue, NW. This building, designed by A.M. Pringle and Bedford Brown IV in 1935, is a clear-cut and symmetrical box with differently proportioned windows on each floor. On the second and third floors, slab and columns disappear behind a sparkling skin of glass brick, and even the interior offices were built with glass. As James Goode has remarked, this central portion of the building "floated in a wall of light." Surrounding the central portion was a sleek façade of enamelled metal panels in white, with decorative details in brilliant yellow and green. An eclectic note was established in the lintels of the second-floor windows, which featured water lily

Even the interiors of the Manhattan Laundry at 1326 Florida Avenue, NW, featured glass brick. The otherwise sedate executive and stenographer pictured above are partaking of the latest architectural "sensation" of the 1930s. (Courtesy Columbia Historical Society)

motifs of an Art Nouveau character, as well as the framing of the entrance, which reflected a classical Greek-Key design. The Manhattan Laundry sits abandoned in one of Washington's poorer neighborhoods, a victim of vandals and fire. Plans for its adaptive reuse, however, have been discussed, and its future looks moderately hopeful.

Other fine examples of industrial Deco buildings using glass brick are the Canada Dry bottling plant in Silver Spring (1201 East-West Highway), designed by the New York architect Walter Monroe Cory in 1946, and the recently demolished Goodwill Industries building at 1217/19 K Street, NW.

Among the "purest" industrial buildings in an urban center are its parking garages. The earliest and the largest in Washington was the enormous Capital Garage on New York Avenue, close to the White House. Designed by Arthur B. Heaton and constructed in 1926, it was built to accommodate 1,200 cars. The enormous bulk facing New York Avenue was broken up into three sections. Stylistically a rather neutral building, the Capital Garage nonetheless displayed prototypical Deco features, especially its low-relief sculptures of automotive details, which anticipated those of the Chrysler Building, and its sculptures of wire-wheeled flivvers bearing 1926 license plates. The building was dynamited in 1974.

In the early 1930s, a parking garage was proposed for the corner of L and 12th Streets, NW, by the firm of Lee, Smith and Vandervoort. The design was fully Deco with its sweeping verticality, jazzy forms, and elaborate spandrels. While this building project was never realized, a quite remarkable Deco parking garage was built in 1940 for the Evening Star Newspaper Company, at 422 10th Street NW. The architects, Porter and Lockie, turned to the studio of John Joseph Earley for the construction of prefabricated panels. As always, the impeccable quality of Earley's panels is visible forty years later.

The Star Parking Plaza, with its distinct tan color and unique treatment of details, was a splendid example of low-level Deco design, and it received the Washington Board of Trade's award as the outstanding structure completed in Washington in 1940. The building's unity flowed from the way in which functional requirements were translated into design solutions: first, light and air were provided by perforated panels—panels that were otherwise identical to those not perforated; second, the lintels above the entrances were reduced in length by the corbelling of the supports; and third, the junction at the split level caused by the d'Humy ramp system was bridged by a vertical shaft element. In less technical terms, the Star Parking Plaza was yet another aesthetic triumph for John Joseph Earley. Its sensitive details were thoroughly Art Deco, and so was the beautiful "Broadway" style of lettering that spelled out the name of the building.

Though the Star Parking Plaza was demolished in 1984, Charles Meyer, a craftsman who worked for the Earley studio, voluntarily salvaged a number of the Earley panels for the Art Deco Society of Washington to donate to a museum.

Among the nation's most exciting and dynamic streamlined buildings of the thirties were the Greyhound bus terminals: "motor transport" beckoned to the passerby in almost every detail. Washington's Greyhound Terminal, built in 1939 at New York Avenue and 11th Street, NW, was one of the finest. The architect William Arrasmith, of the Louisville firm of Wischmeyer, Arrasmith and Elswick, designed at least fifteen other Greyhound terminals across the country.

In 1940 the Evening Star Newspaper Company commissioned Porter and Lockie to design this parking garage around the corner from the newspaper's Pennsylvania Avenue offices. The architects in turn subcontracted the exterior panels to the J.J. Earley studio. The resulting ventilated façade was referred to as a "lace curtain of concrete" in the trade journals.

This side view of the 1940 Star Parking Plaza shows that the ziggurat motif remained the mode for certain architects long after the 1930s streamline vogue developed.

Circa 1970, the graceful lines of the 1940 Greyhound Terminal of Washington were still visible. Some six years later, the Greyhound Corporation renovated the building by virtually encasing it in cement-asbestos panels with a huge mansard roof. The original building, however, is still intact beneath the brutalist superstructure. (Courtesy Richard Longstreth).

Almost every corner of the Washington terminal was rounded in an effort to convey the excitement of speed. The façade was constructed of limestone with black terra-cotta trim. But the crowning touch was the central tower, surmounted, as James Goode has said, "by a speeding chrome greyhound." The circular waiting room looked out upon the rear loading platform and opened out into restaurants. One of the prime examples of late streamline Art Deco buildings in Washington, this excellent structure was defaced in 1976 with a squat mansard roof, hiding all the qualities of its architecture, including the very emblem of the firm—the greyhound.[29]

On a happier note, there exists (safely ensconced on a grassy suburban site) a remarkable semi-industrial Deco building in nearby Wheaton, Maryland. A radio transmitter, its streamlined Deco design reflects an architectural ideal of Le Corbusier: "The wise play of volumes in sunlight and shade." The crisp lines of the WTOP transmitter on University Boulevard, designed by E. Burton Corning in 1939, have more in common with a house by Richard Neutra in California or a building in the Weissenhof-Siedlung of Stuttgart than with most of the other Art Deco in the city of Washington. Nonetheless, they reflect the most popular, expressive elements of streamline Art Deco as a nationwide vogue, including the extensive use of glass brick.

An apotheosis of streamlining, the radio transmitting station of WTOP in Wheaton, Maryland, was the work of local architect E. Burton Corning. In 1939 the structure was the brand-new facility of station WJSV.

Movie Theaters

It was not until the early 1930s that the first consistently Deco theaters were built in American cities. The picture palaces of the 1920s—from small theaters in country towns to theaters of the size of New York City's Roxy, which seated 6,000—were invariably built in eclectic combinations of traditional styles. Movie houses carried on the ephemeral but vastly effective tradition of the early music halls and fairground booths until the Crash of 1929 put an end to the more voluptuous trends of 1920s design, and a crisper style took over. Until then, Renaissance, Byzantine, Neo-Baroque, Roman, French, Spanish, Moorish, Persian, Chinese, and a welter of namelessly exotic forms were displayed in American cinemas.

Among the leading cinema architects were Thomas Lamb of New York, whose work was firmly rooted in the Beaux Arts school, and Austrian-born John Eberson, whose so-called "atmospheric" theaters were flamboyant contrasts to Lamb's more conservative designs. The architectural firms of George and C. W. Rapp and C. Howard Crane occupied the middle ground.

In the early thirties, theater designers were consciously drawn to an array of styles

The illuminated glass tower of the Trans-Lux Theater was the largest of its kind in the world, according to the Trans-Lux Corporation. This cinema was part of the firm's network of newsreel theaters throughout the East Coast. Images were projected from behind the screen instead of across the auditorium. (Courtesy Richard Longstreth)

more in keeping with the "modern age." Goaded by critics like P. Morton Shand, whose *Modern Theaters and Cinemas*, published in 1930, pleaded with designers for "modernist settings for film scenarios of the type with which 'Metropolis' has familiarized us"[30] (he referred to the futuristic visions in the 1926 film), and inspired by Donald Deskey's outstanding work in Radio City Music Hall in 1932, designers like Eberson, Lamb, and Rapp & Rapp started to produce a line of picture palaces suited to the age of Harlow, Astaire and Rogers, and Busby Berkeley: thoroughly Deco cinemas.

The big palaces, however, were now giving way to smaller units, which reflected the lower expectations of Depression-era moviegoers. In design, the change was rather positive: a new symbiosis of function and contemporary decoration was leading to a glamorous display of Deco in a classic genre.

Yet cultural and economic changes have left the Deco movie palaces threatened and neglected. Though a number of these structures remain in Washington, a larger number have been altered beyond recognition, abandoned, or destroyed. The most grievous loss was the streamlined Trans-Lux cinema. Words can do little justice to the beauty of the building designed by Thomas Lamb and constructed in 1936 on the corner of 14th Street and New York Avenue, NW. In the dedication of the newsletter bearing its name, the Art Deco Society of Washington describes it thus:

Grievously smashed to the ground in 1975, the stunning Trans-Lux Theater of 1936 would rank today among the finest Art Deco buildings in Washington. Designed by cinema architect Thomas Lamb, the theater was called a "delight to the eye" on its opening night by the *Evening Star's* reporter Jay Carmody. (Courtesy Richard Longstreth)

The theater swept down the block like an ocean liner, with a prismatic mirror tower on one end and an RCA radio transmitter with thunderbolt script on the other.[31]

Truly, the building was one of Washington's most elegant Art Deco buildings, a delightful composition of sweeping horizontality and vertical elements, the crystalline look of the extraordinary glass tower, the wavelike stretching of the marquee, the interior murals by Andres Hudiakoff, which Michael Kernan remembers depicting "cowboys and horses and clouds."[32] Offices and shops were included in the complex building, which boasted one of Washington's first air-conditioned theaters devoted to showing newsreels.[33]

The Trans-Lux theater was the only Art Deco design that Lamb produced in Washington. Of his earlier theaters from the twenties—the Ambassador and Palace and Tivoli—only the latter survives. Among the other out-of-town theater designers of national

Another lost Deco theater, the Reed, was demolished at 1723 King Street in Alexandria, Virginia, several years ago. The Reed was designed by the Baltimore firm of John J. Zink and completed in 1936. Zink and his arch-competitor John Eberson were each responsible for designing around a dozen Deco theaters in the Washington area. Most have been destroyed. (Courtesy Theatre Historical Society)

stature, perhaps the most important was John Eberson, who built at least thirteen of the important Deco theaters in Washington, establishing a presence that was almost equaled by his Baltimore rival, John J. Zink, who designed at least eleven. Both Eberson and Zink created theaters that blended congenially with the Deco structures designed by Washington architects.[34]

Newspaper sources reveal that most of the Deco theaters designed by Eberson and Zink in Washington were part of a general program of construction sponsored by the Warner Brothers movie chain. John J. Payette, the general zone manager for Warner's, oversaw the construction of most of the theaters and sponsored the gala events at the opening of neighborhood movie houses, events where District of Columbia Commissioners and civic association leaders were usually present.

Eberson's most remarkable theater is the Penn on Capitol Hill (644 Pennsylvania Avenue, SE). The entire building—the entrance, marquee, frontage, and the main body of the structure—merges into architectural unity through the use of the same tan color in bricks, limestone, plasterwork, and trim. Even the tension inherent in its volumetric treatment—the rounded marquee and the clear-cut box of the main façade—bespeaks a spectacular blending of rectilinear and curvilinear planes. The flowing marquee is the streamline style at its most exuberant, and its sweeping form contrasts in almost perfect proportion to the dignified ornamentation of the façade with its three slightly recessed decorative insets. Completed in 1935, the Penn has recently been adapted to a mixed-use proposal by architect David Schwarz.

Eberson's other movie houses in Washington are slightly more modest in conception. The Sheridan and Atlantic theaters (6225 Georgia Avenue, NW, and 21 Atlantic Street,

SW) feature interestingly patterned walls with jagged, recessed, or colored brick courses along with a standard metal marquee. A playful detail is incorporated in the Highland Theater (2533 Pennsylvania Avenue, SE), which is now badly damaged by fire. Above the colorful Vitrolite-framed entranceway are vertical rows of alternating tan and black brickwork recalling the sprocket holes of the films projected inside.

Eberson's most productive rival in Washington was John J. Zink of the Baltimore architectural firm of Zink, Atkins, and Craycroft. The acknowledged regional specialist in movie houses, this firm built more than 200 theaters in Baltimore, New York, Washington, and other eastern cities. Zink was a particularly versatile designer; each of his buildings was different, and all were very well adapted to particular site conditions. The entrances of two theaters with corner locations are placed at the angles of turning, and the entire buildings accentuate the pivotal corner. At the Langston Theater, a late-Deco structure of 1945 (2501 Benning Road, NE), the side walls swing out at the corner forming two heavy pilasterlike towers beside the recessed entrance. The whole building mass of the Langston is dissolved into a handsome interplay of streamlined shapes, rectangular volumes, and zigzag cornice lines. At the Newton, an earlier theater of 1937 in the Brookland neighborhood (3601 12th Street, NW), the entrance and marquee are topped with a delightful and simple metal sculpture containing both the name and the symbolic Deco fountain motif.

Zink's larger movie houses, such as the Uptown Theater of 1936 and the MacArthur Theater of 1946, are necessarily bulkier than his neighborhood theaters. Nonetheless,

One of the earliest and finest of the Washington Deco theaters designed by the New York firm of John Eberson, the Penn, on Capitol Hill, was completed in 1935. Another Eberson theater nearby, the Beverly (now demolished), featured the same ribbed marquee. The street façade of the Penn will be adapted to a mixed-use project designed by architect David Schwarz. (Courtesy Maxwell MacKenzie)

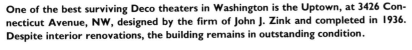

he achieved in them all a harmonious articulation of façades, breaking the scale by means of alternating terra cotta and brick and by introducing fluted panels and projected, recessed, or colored brick course. On the large, symmetrical frontage of the Uptown Theater especially, this made for a quiet but significant Art Deco façade.

Washington's theaters did not reflect the general trend of transition within the Art Deco style from the jazzy forms of the twenties to the later emphasis on streamline. On the contrary, hard-edged zigzag lines can be found on Deco theaters of the late thirties and early forties as frequently as they appeared upon the earliest Deco theaters in town, such as the Circle (2105 Pennsylvania Avenue NW), remodeled in 1932 with a terraced roofline. This was also true of the remarkably well-proportioned Apex Theater, designed by Zink in 1940 and demolished in 1977 (4813 Massachusetts Avenue, NW). The strong symmetry was underscored by the four-fold terracing upon the marquee, which was done in accentuating monochromatic shades of blue, and by the twin medallions flanking the central portion, which depicted Egyptian goddesses—a classic 1920s image held over into 1940.

Again, the feelings of the twenties and thirties combine in the Atlas Theater (1329–31 H Street, NE), designed by Zink in 1939 and badly damaged in the 1968 riots. The zigzag pattern is prominently used on the marquee, and the steamlined forms of the main façade are ingeniously arranged through the staggering of three terra-cotta slabs, assembled into one of the only asymmetrical Deco theater façades in the city. This sculptural blending of zigzag and streamline forms makes the Atlas rank among the finest Art Deco façades in Washington.

Many typical Deco cinema lobbies and auditoriums have been altered beyond rec-

Opening night at the Apex Theater in 1940 featured *Down Argentine Way* with Carmen Miranda and Don Ameche. The theater, perhaps the most successful design by Zink's firm in Washington, was situated in the affluent neighborhood of Spring Valley on Massachusetts Avenue, NW. It was destroyed in 1977 and replaced with an almost featureless brick building. (Courtesy Columbia Historical Society)

One of the finest surviving Eberson movie theaters in the Washington area is this one: the Silver Theater in the Maryland suburb of Silver Spring. The sleek, white tower above the marquee sweeps back to a nautically influenced auditorium adorned with a porthole window and dark horizontal pinstripe bands. The theater is itself the anchor of a shopping center, also designed by the firm of Eberson, creating a block-long harmony of streamlines. (Courtesy Herbert Striner)

ognition or have fallen into disrepair. An excellent exception is the lobby of the Senator Theater (3950 Minnesota Avenue, NE), designed by Zink in 1942 with a colorful exterior trim and a stunningly elegant lobby that remains in fine condition.[35] Yet another notable Deco lobby (with an elegant aluminum ticket booth) was created as a later addition to the Warner Theater, originally designed by C. Howard Crane in the early twenties.

Outside the city of Washington proper, a number of Deco movie houses were built in the thirties and early forties, the finest being the Bethesda and Silver theaters, respectively in Bethesda and Silver Spring, Maryland, both designed by the firm of John Eberson. Both differ from Washington theaters, except for the lost Trans-Lux, in their centerpiece: the rising tower. The tower above the marquee of the Bethesda Theater (7719 Wisconsin Avenue) is a beautifully proportioned metal sculpture with articulated base and top, with the middle shaft holding the letters of its name. The tower is so consistently designed that it could almost have served as an architectural prototype model for skyscraper building at the World's Fairs at Chicago in 1933 and New York in 1939. The tower of the Silver Theater (8619 Colesville Road) is different from that of any other theater in the region. With the lower part swinging out from the roof of the lobby, the tower conveys the feeling of a white, nautical, water-streamlined object. The nautical feeling is continued in the beautifully patterned brick striping of the auditorium, which, in turn, harmonizes with the streamlined adjacent shopping center, also designed by Eberson's firm for the multimillionaire developer William Alexander Julian in 1938. This combination of movie theater and shopping center design was hailed as a national milestone in trade journals.

Such were the Deco theaters of Washington, theaters on the whole more modest in design than elsewhere across the country, but remarkable, chiefly, for their stunning variety of forms.

Sports Halls and Amusement Parks

Recreational buildings combined the most flamboyant and functional aspects of Art Deco, and in the case of the little-known gymnasium and roller-skating rink—America On Wheels—on Kalorama Road, the combination is striking. This large gymnasium, built in the mid-1940s, is unobtrusive, displaying its function in a clear dialogue of volumes and structural system, yet it serves as a remarkable example of late streamline aesthetics. Special treatment was given to the main entrance where steps, columns, and horizontal and vertical slabs formed a rather cubistic setting. The building was designed by Frank Grad and Company.

More whimsically expressive were the buildings designed in the thirties for the noted amusement park, Glen Echo. Dating to the 1890s, the park displays structures of several epochs, but the most important are those of the 1930s, when Glen Echo reached its peak of popularity. Connected to downtown Washington by a streetcar line, and thus a magnet for summertime weekend crowds, the park was formally closed in 1968, but a number of streamline Deco structures remain. The streetcar station and park entrance, the popcorn stand, the "Arcade," the rides like "Laugh in the Dark" and "Cuddle-Up" are period pieces of streamline design in colors associated with seaside resorts: white, pastel green, and ocean blue.

The structures from the early thirties like the Crystal Pool (1931) and the Spanish Ballroom (1933) were more formal than the later fanciful creations. The Spanish Ballroom was distinctly derived from the popular ballrooms of the twenties. The Philadelphia architectural firm of Alexander, Becker, and Schoeppe was responsible for designing most of the Deco structures in the park.[36] Since 1976, Glen Echo Amusement Park has been maintained by the National Park Service, which is nominating five of the Deco structures for inclusion in the National Register of Historic Places.

Throughout the 1930s, federal architecture reflected the battle between traditionalists and radical modernists, with Art Deco being used as a form of compromise. From openly classical buildings like the one designed for the Supreme Court to the housing designed along the lines of the International Style for Greenbelt, federal architecture ran the gamut of contending styles. But most of the federal buildings designed in the years of Hoover and FDR were of the "stripped classical" lines that reflected the compromise formula proposed by *The Federal Architect* in 1930—"The Moderne traditionalized, the Traditional modernized"—with Art Deco fitting in through the mode of "Greco-Deco" embellishments.

Stripped classical prevailed in almost every instance, at times to the exclusion of Deco. In 1935, for example, the competition for a Federal Reserve Board building brought forth a variety of entries in the Beaux Arts style. Only the entry of Holabird and Root bore reference to Art Deco, and the winning entry, by Paul Philippe Cret, subsequently built, contained not a single modernistic detail, though Cret designed many Deco buildings, among them the Deco-inclined Folger Shakespeare Library and the superb Deco Hall of Science at the 1933 Chicago World's Fair.

Nevertheless, in three of the buildings constructed in the Federal Triangle, Art Deco is in evidence. In the Post Office Building designed by William Adams Delano, mild, prototypical hints of Art Deco began to infiltrate the more traditionally classical features, particularly in the Deco-tending chandelier in the Postmaster-General's Reception Room and in the long spiral staircase for which the building is widely noted.

Far more explicit were the Deco features of the Justice Department Building. Indeed this building is one of the finest examples of "Greco-Deco" in Washington. Deco features abound throughout the Justice Department Building, from the lighting fixtures and decorative doors and gates to the beautiful Deco lamps in the law library. The entrance, vestibule, and lobby at the northwest corner of the building were done in a "high style" Deco manner with polished marble, fine metalwork, and color mosaics by John Joseph Earley. Other masterworks by Earley can be found on the ceiling above the driveway on the mid-block entrance on 10th Street. These extraordinary polychrome ceilings represent the Earley genius at its best, and they rank among the finest examples of his work to be found in the city. The colors remains exquisite, from a sandy yellow to a dominant deep blue, evoking the feeling of a fairy tale sky. But the ceilings were not only decorative embellishments. At the direction of the building's architects—the Philadelphia firm of Zantzinger, Borie and Medary—the precast concrete slabs were prepared as a mold for the structural concrete floor above, an entirely new concept in building that served to guarantee permanence.[37]

Aside from the Earley ceilings, noteworthy Deco design can be found in the Justice Department's auditorium, in which beautiful Deco motifs abound in aluminum moldings and trim. Especially fine are the Deco chandelier and silvered plasterwork adorning the ceiling of the elevator lobby directly behind the auditorium. All the aluminum trim, along with aluminum statues of Deco gods and goddesses displayed in the auditorium, was evidently the work of the neoclassical sculptor C. Paul Jennewein. The architects commissioned the sculptor to supervise the ornamental treatment throughout the building; the metalwork was done by the firm of Edward F. Caldwell and Company in New York City.

Two blocks to the east of the Department of Justice, the building designed for the Federal Trade Commission reflects a more subdued application of Art Deco details. Completed in 1937 by the firm of Bennett, Parsons & Frost, the Federal Trade Commission Building is a streamlined version of stripped classical, an "aerodynamic" columned

Ornate Deco is the spirit of the elevator lobby behind the Justice Department's main auditorium. Aluminum Deco railings, designed to the specifications of sculptor C. Paul Jennewein, are topped by the ceiling ornamentation of silvered plasterwork on a rich blue background. (Courtesy Day Walters)

wedge that forms the tip of the Federal Triangle. Heroic New Deal sculptures of wild horses being tamed by muscular heroes flank the building, which is virtually devoid of Art Deco details, with a spectacular exception—the doors. These splendid aluminum gates are emblazoned with ocean liners and clipper planes in melodramatic perspectives. The sculptor was William McVey.

In only a few of the New Deal government buildings was the balance between "Greco" and "Deco" tipped in favor of the latter. In the Justice Department Building, Deco's pervasive presence is teasingly subdued, and in the case of the Federal Trade Commission Building, it is largely confined to the entrance. Another entrance of predominantly Art Deco design involving doors, sidings, and canopy appears on the General Accounting Office Building (441 G Street, NW), erected in the Truman years and designed by Gilbert Stanley Underwood. The sculpture on both sides of the entrance follows the sweeping curves of the marble facing, and the long, abbreviated canopy is trimmed with Greek-Key ornaments and eagles.

A dramatic frontal view of an ocean liner, a Deco image made popular in dozens of travel posters, is featured in the ornamental aluminum gates of the Federal Trade Commission Building in the Federal Triangle. The sculptor was William McVey.

Though completed in the Truman era, the Deco spirit lingers in the bas-relief ornamentation of the General Accounting Office building at 441 G Street, NW. The sculptor was Joseph Kiselewski.

Yet another federal building with Deco traces is the semi-industrial Central Heating and Refrigeration Plant (13th and C Streets, NW), designed by Paul Cret in collaboration with James A. Wetmore of the Treasury Department's Office of the Supervising Architect. Tucked away behind more visible government buildings, the plant is a functionalistic structure of massive bulk with vertical window shafts between buttresslike brick pilasters. On the main façade are randomly interspersed Deco bas-relief sculptures of mechanical details done in terra cotta and limestone. Cret's design for the plant is a good illustration of a heavy industrial Deco building whose stolidity contrasts to the later streamlined forms of the Hecht's warehouse.

Aside from these Deco touches and traces, there exists in the federal enclave an absolute masterpiece of Art Deco design: the 1939 Library of Congress Annex, originally named for Thomas Jefferson but recently renamed for John Adams. The calm and flowing Greco-Deco exterior of the building, designed by the firm of Pierson and Wilson, is perfectly adapted to its site. The façades, with their stepped-back upper stories, relate chivalrously both to the main Library of Congress building across the street and the adjoining delicate form of the Folger Shakespeare Library. Slight, sandblasted ornamental friezes around the entrance doors and pediment contribute to the crisp appearance of this bright marble structure. On the shorter side of the building on Independence Avenue, a sculptured stairway, flanked with superb carvings and elaborate lamps, leads up to the second-floor entrance.

But the true glories are within. In the vestibule, lobby, and halls of the first floor,

A streamlined owl stands watch at the southern entrance of the 1939 Annex to the Library of Congress. The stripped classical styling is rich in Deco ornamentation, which has prompted the recent appellation "Greco-Deco."

Plant motif in elaborate Deco metalwork adorns the vestibule of the 1939 Library of Congress Annex. Most of this ornamental trim was produced by the Flour City Ornamental Iron Company, Minneapolis.

and in the elevator lobby, corridors, reading rooms, and chambers of the fifth floor, an abundance of Art Deco at its most ornate is a perfect refutation of the view that the styles of the 1925 Paris exposition can be banned from assessments of 1930s design. Here, in a 1939 structure, is Art Deco in its Aztec-derived mode. Plant motifs that repeat themselves upon doors, water fountains, walls, and unpredictable surfaces make this a thoroughly intriguing example of Deco interior design. Every essential chamber is fully wainscoted with a careful selection of figured marble and stone and a wealth of metal reliefs. The elevator doors are outstanding examples of the sensitive craftsmanship reflected throughout the building. This ornamental design was largely the work of sculptor Lee Lawrie, who supervised the metalwork done by the Flour City Ornamental Iron Company of Minneapolis. Aside from the abundance of detail, the building has streamlined office corridors around the fifth-floor reading rooms that seem to be taken directly from the sleekest Pullman-car designs of the age. This returns us to the question: can zigzag and streamline be severed when they clearly combine in a building from the late 1930s?

No efforts were spared to make the annex as efficient as possible. Among its modern features were conveyor belts and pneumatic tubes for transporting books and an extensive use of Formica, which earned the architects an award in a national plastics competition.[38] The two main reading rooms of simple and elegant design feature murals by Ezra Winter,

The lofty white tower of Bethesda Naval Hospital has long been a familiar sight on the outskirts of Bethesda, Maryland. Exempt from the District of Columbia's height limitation, the building is thus a rare Washingtonian example of the Deco skyscraper style.

the artist who produced the extraordinary Art Deco mural in New York's Radio City Music Hall in 1932.

The Library of Congress Annex is the best and richest government Art Deco building in Washington. With the outbreak of World War II, the design of government buildings became austere, though retaining vestigial Deco touches. Three buildings in the metropolitan area were typical of this trend: the U.S. Naval Medical Center in Bethesda, Maryland, the David W. Taylor Model Basin at Carderock, Maryland, and the Washington National Airport across the Potomac in Virginia. The twenty-two-story medical center, sometimes referred to as Washington's first skyscraper, features lower wings with a soaring tower in the center. The height—unusual for Washington—is further emphasized by vertical window shafts and gradual setbacks. Though rumor has it that the center's original conception was in part the work of President Roosevelt, the architects of record were F.W. Southworth and Paul Philippe Cret. To a large extent, this design was inspired by Bertram Goodhue's pioneering work on the Nebraska State Capitol building and shows as well the obvious influence of 1930s skyscrapers.

Mildly Art Deco are the Taylor Model Basin (where models of naval vessels are tested in wind tunnels) and the Washington National Airport. The main terminal building is part of the airport's gently curving facilities, linked like a string of pearls by a sheltering cement canopy. The colonnaded central building makes use of a few Deco features, such as concrete mosaics and glass etchings of American eagles in the windows facing the runway. The outlying hangars give a sense of what "aerodrome" meant in the age of Antoine de St. Exupéry, with their flaring sides and interior lights aglow.

Municipal Structures

The Municipal Center of the District of Columbia government (300 Indiana Avenue, NW) is perhaps the most perfect example of "Greco-Deco" public buildings in the city. Its overall classical appearance features flat, pilastered façades with vertical fenestration. At a closer look, a multitude of Deco details are apparent in the abstracted bas-reliefs of Corinthian capitals flanking the windows above the entrance and the cast-aluminum

Weather symbols in aluminum are part of the decorative pattern of Washington's Municipal Center designed by Nathan C. Wyeth. Sunray and thunderbolt patterns were staples of Deco design in both the 1920s and 1930s.

A Wagnerian goddess racing a thirties automobile is one of four Deco sculptures by Leon Hermant on the Calvert Street Bridge, which was recently renamed for Duke Ellington. The bridge was designed by Cret and completed in 1935. Ancient deities and modern technology were frequently combined in Deco imagery, perhaps as a form of historical commentary.

This jazzy Deco railing is part of the Klingle Valley Bridge on Connecticut Avenue above the Kennedy-Warren. The bridge, designed by Paul Philippe Cret and Frank M. Masters and built in 1931, features classical-tending urns of fluted glass.

elements above the doors that serve as spandrels. The consistently Deco patterning utilized corrugated "swell-front" panels, stylized plant motifs, sunray and thunderbolt patterns, in a series of excellent combinations. The lobby of the building has a splendid floor in which a map of the city is rendered in a combination of terrazzo and mosaic.

The building, completed in 1941, was the work of Nathan C. Wyeth, municipal architect from 1934 to 1946. Wyeth (1870–1963), trained at the Ecole des Beaux Arts in Paris before the turn of the century, was chief designer for the Architect of the Capitol in 1904 and 1905. He was later responsible for designing a number of palatial residences and embassy buildings. His second large Deco-tending building was the District of Columbia Armory (2001 East Capitol Street, NE), completed the same year as the District's Municipal Center. The Armory combines the calmness of Wyeth's classical style with an obvious Deco and streamline flair.

Two other municipal structures reflected the influence of Art Deco, both of them bridges designed by that versatile genius Paul Philippe Cret. The Connecticut Avenue Bridge over Klingle Valley, completed in 1931, perfectly complements the style of the Kennedy-Warren apartment building, which was erected immediately south of the bridge the following year. Jazzy railings and fluted-glass urns are familiar landmarks through which the bridge thematically connects the Kennedy-Warren to the block of Deco buildings featuring the Uptown Theater. Cret's second Deco bridge was the Calvert Street Bridge, recently renamed for Duke Ellington. Completed in 1935, this bold, massive structure featured three arches of concrete construction faced with Indiana limestone. Pylons flanking the entrances bear sculptures of Deco gods and goddesses by sculptor Leon Hermant, the finest of which depicts a thoroughly Wagnerian goddess of speed, racing a streamlined car.

The exquisite form of the Folger Shakespeare Library, designed by Cret and completed in 1932, epitomized the "modern traditionalized, the traditional modernized." Synthesized in the powerful but delicate design are some of the important tendencies of 1930s design: simplification of form, streamlined surfaces, classical antecedents, and Art Deco ornamentation in railings and grillwork.

Educational Buildings

Paul Philippe Cret (1876–1945), that master of Greco-Deco design, was the architect of one of the finest educational and cultural buildings in the city, the 1932 Folger Shakespeare Library. Born in Lyon, Cret attended the Ecole des Beaux Arts in both Lyon and Paris, and came to the United States early in the twentieth century to accept a position as professor of design at the University of Pennsylvania. He left academia in 1907 to establish his own firm. The Folger Library helped solidify his position as a champion of the principles expounded in the pages of *The Federal Architect*, principles of mediation between the classical revival gaining ground in the twenties and the irrepressible power of modernism.

Cret was too individual an artist to apply a superficially modern look to a basically traditional structure. The quiet, harmoniously classic proportions of the Folger Library bespeak a very modern design that does not repudiate the past. Its modern feeling is reflected in the rhythmic pattern of its windows and closed walls, the proportion of pediment to lower façade, the creative use of cast aluminum for structural and decorative purposes in fenestration, grilles, and railings. The designer's purpose was revealed in his own declaration in 1925 that a "new classicism, achieving beauty through good proportions rather than through the picturesque, will be born" as a result of impatience with static tradition.[39]

While the Folger Library building typified Greco-Deco, another hybrid style was developed in the late thirties on the campus of George Washington University in five new halls and in the Lisner Auditorium, designed in 1942. Most of the buildings were designed by Washington architect Waldron Faulkner. Their style was a variation of Art

Lisner Hall, designed by Waldron Faulker, glows in an almost supernatural light in this pencil rendering by illustrator Hugh Ferriss, whose most famous book, *The Metropolis of Tomorrow*, published in 1929 (perhaps inspired by the visions of Fritz Lang's film *Metropolis* in 1926), showed futuristic visions of sculpted skyscraper forms in melodramatic settings. (The George Washington University Permanent Collection, courtesy of the Dimock Gallery)

Superb bas-relief sculptures of scenes from the Shakespeare plays are flanked by streamlined fluted columns on the front façade of the Folger Library.

Deco very close to the forms of the International Style—but not quite. Efficient use of materials and space was the guiding principle, but clear decoration remained. Faulkner (1898–1979) was born in Paris and educated at Yale, where he graduated with a Bachelor of Fine Arts degree in 1924. While at Yale, Faulkner was awarded a student medal by the American Institute of Architects (AIA), and after practicing architecture in New York he moved to Washington, founding the firm of Faulkner and Kingsbury. The buildings he designed for George Washington University at 21st and G streets, NW, were modern enough to prompt the Museum of Modern Art in New York to request photographs of Lisner Hall, Stuart Hall, Bell Hall, and the Hall of Government for the museum's collection on nineteenth- and twentieth-century architecture.

The centerpiece of this late 1930s group of buildings is Lisner Hall (formerly the University library). Flanked by the lower, horizontal Stuart and Bell Halls, the short tower of Lisner marks the visual axis for the university's quadrangle.

For the purpose of fundraising on behalf of the university's trustees, Faulkner commissioned the eminent artist Hugh Ferriss, the author of *The Metropolis of Tomorrow* and an artist he had known from his days of architectural practice in New York, to produce two architectural renderings. One of the drawings, in Ferriss's inimitable style, survives; it depicts graduation day in front of Lisner Hall's north façade, bathed in an exquisite play of light and shade.

Among the other notable Deco buildings designed for educational purposes are George

Washington Jr. High School in Alexandria, Virginia, designed by Virginia State School Division architect Raymond Long in 1935 in a vibrant Deco spirit, and the building designed as a showpiece of Greenbelt, Maryland, the Greenbelt Center School. This stunning creation served as both the town's elementary school and civic center, and its beauty was unsurpassed by the later, more conservative Greenbelt Middle School built further west along Greenbelt Road near Berwyn Heights.

Greenbelt Center School is the finest streamlined Art Deco educational structure in the region—and perhaps the country. Designed in 1936 by architects Douglas Ellington and Reginald D. Wadsworth, it served as a stylistic point of departure from the ultra-rational principles inherent in the rest of the New Deal town. Whereas the residential buildings, and even the airy and streamlined pedestrian mall at the town center, owed much to the International Style, the Center School is almost sensuous. Streamlined, fluted, and aerodynamic-looking struts adorn the sides, curving walls define the entrance,

This solidly Deco high school building of 1935 was designed by architects retained by the state of Virginia. George Washington High School (now in service as a junior high school) is located in Alexandria. (Courtesy Jack Masarsky)

99

The exuberant lines of Greenbelt Center Elementary School were perhaps inspired by Cret's design for the Folger Shakespeare Library. Bas-relief sculpture is employed in the same position on the 1936 building, flanked by fluted columns in the form of streamlined fins. The architects, Douglas Ellington and Reginald D. Wadsworth, designed the building to serve as both school and community center in the New Deal model town. (Courtesy Herbert Striner)

and intersecting volumes provide this school with a rare architectural quality: this is a delightfully *pleasant* building. Bas-relief sculptures of common men at the base-line—inspired, perhaps, by the similar use of sculpture by Cret in the Folger Shakespeare Library—spell out the preamble to the Constitution in "We, the People" terms that evoke the spirit of John Steinbeck and Woody Guthrie in the mind of the observer. The sculptures were the work of Lenore Thomas.

Social and Religious Buildings

Among the various types of buildings affected by Art Deco, churches were the "least and the latest." Conscious of powerful tradition, architects were hesitant to stray beyond inherited forms. It was not until the mid-1940s that modern design began to infiltrate American ecclesiastical architecture to any significant degree.

There are, however, a few noteworthy exceptions in Washington. One of the earliest, a college and monastery built by the order of Franciscan Friars of the Holy Name Province in 1930, was one of several religious and educational institutions affiliated with Catholic University. The Franciscans commissioned architect Chester Oakley to design a building rich in ecclesiastical ornamentation. The result was an eclectic building with important features of Art Deco, especially in the terra-cotta ornamentation and the use of buttresslike columns as pedestals from which emerge the sculpted figures of saints. Another important, if less flamboyant religious building with Art Deco elements, is located on Capitol Hill directly across from the Folger Shakespeare Library.

The Lutheran Church of the Reformation on East Capitol Street, completed as early

ESTABLISH JUSTICE

The spirit of New Deal populism suffuses the bas-relief sculptures of Greenbelt Center Elementary School. The panels, sculpted in place on the building by Lenore Thomas, a WPA artist, spell out the clauses of the Constitution's Preamble, starting with "We The People." The proletarian spirit of such "Social Realist" art was at times heavily fraught with romantic idealism. (Courtesy Herbert Striner)

as 1934 by the firm of Porter and Lockie, represents the finest surviving building designed by this firm in the Deco style. The senior partner in the firm, Irwin Stevens Porter (1889–1957), was born in Washington and attended George Washington University. He served as an apprentice of the classicist Waddy Wood, and he later became president of the Washington chapter of AIA. The work of Porter and Lockie in the thirties was a dignified Washington version of Art Deco that was heavily reliant on the products of the J.J. Earley studio.

The keynote feature of the Lutheran Church of the Reformation is the limestone relief above the entrance, where the central figure of Christ is the merging point for the alignment of all other figures arranged in a fanlike pattern.

Similarly, the centerpiece of the Scottish Rite Temple on 16th Street, designed by Porter, Lockie, and Chatelain in 1939, is a highly decorative panel above the main door. The extraordinarily rich polychrome panel was again the work of the Earley studio. The sunburst pattern represents what is probably Earley's most sophisticated, intricate work in Washington. In the center of the pattern and to both sides of the panel and door, elaborate copper and white metal ornaments add to the strength of expression of this outstanding entrance.

Farther north is the B'Nai Israel Synagogue, designed by Maurice Courland in 1946 (4606 16th Street, NW). Traditional elements merge into a subtle expression of subdued streamline aesthetics. A similar streamlined church, the Sligo Seventh-Day Adventist Church, designed by J. Raymond Mims and completed in 1944, can be found in the suburban recesses of Takoma Park, Maryland. The depressed arches of the entrance arcade and the side-door lintels are the only departures from the pure streamline design of the building, with its setback cornice lines wrapping around its façade.

EPILOG

Art Deco did not have a warm reception in Washington; it was not overtly embraced to complement the city's development. In other American cities, Art Deco became the stylistic device par excellence for particular architectural genres: the soaring skyscrapers in New York, the tropical resort architecture in Miami Beach, the self-conscious corporate architecture of oil-booming Tulsa, the streamlined buildings of the automobile city of Los Angeles.

Washington's architecture of the twenties and thirties could not suddenly disentangle itself from a number of prevailing constraints. L'Enfant's powerful baroque plan of 1792 subordinated each building to the given urban pattern. The imposed height limitations prohibited trespassing excesses beyond the building envelope. Furthermore, the tradition of design-controlling commissions, conscious of the dignified image of the Nation's Capital, curtailed any striking departures. Finally, the omnipresence of the classical federal architecture, also universally accepted by the Imperial cities of London, Paris, Vienna, Berlin, and Rome, represented a strong stylistic trendsetter.

However tangible these influences were, the Art Deco movement established itself in the local architectural scene by developing its own constellation. For all its diversity, Washington Art Deco acquired a civic identity. The classical Greco-Deco manifestations, the urbane and elegant Deco apartment buildings, the sober architectural approaches of the New Dealers, the off-street undiluted residential and commercial Deco examples, the ubiquitous influence of local genius in the work of J.J. Earley, all have given the Nation's Capital a heritage of Art Deco that deserves recognition and praise.

Aesthetically, Washington's Deco buildings add a worthy presence to the architecture of the city. They all possess a quality that art critic Benjamin Forgey referred to as a kind of "civility." Elegant civility, combined with expressive and exuberant forms, is a cultural manifestation that might be regarded as Washington's architectural contribution to the Art Deco era in America.

APPENDIX

LIST OF ART DECO BUILDINGS

Note: In cases where no building permit was available, information was derived from the building's owner or from secondary sources. Ⓓ indicates "demolished."

ADDRESS	NAME OF STRUCTURE	USE	ARCHITECT/ DEVELOPER	BUILDING PERMIT NO.	YEAR OF CONSTR.	RESIDENTIAL
300-304 Aspen St., NW (see listing for Whittier St., NW)						**Buildings in District of Columbia—** listed by alphabetical, followed by numerical, streets
4208 Benning Rd., NE		Garden Apts.	Cyril G. Bow, arch. Oliver Cassell, dev.	226055	1939	
4228 Benning Rd., NE		Garden Apts.	R.C. Archer, Jr., arch. Michael Kapnick, dev.	276550	1945	
4236 Benning Rd., NE		Garden Apts.	L.W. Giles, arch. Mildred de Arellano, dev.	273482	1944	
4274 Benning Rd., NE		Garden Apts.	G.T. Santmyers, arch. E.M. Aiken, Inc., dev.	251728	1942	
2300-2308 Benton St., NW (see listing for 42d St., NW)						
120 C St., NE	Senate Courts	Apts.	G.T. Santmyers, arch. Chas. T. Sager, dev.	118384	1928	
3718 Calvert St., NW		Single-Family House	Dillon + Abel, arch. M.J. Kossow, dev.	216231	1938	
3901 Cathedral Ave., NW	The Marlyn	Apts.	Harvey Warwick, arch. (Francis Koenig, assoc.) Gustave Ring, dev.		1938	
5535 Chevy Chase Pkwy., NW		Single-Family House	J.J. Daly, arch. Jos. + Nettie Madigan, dev.	300314	1947	
5610 Colorado Ave., NW		Apts.	G.T. Santmyers, arch. National Construc. Co., dev.	209715	1938	
5746 Colorado Ave., NW		Apts.	G.T. Santmyers, arch. National Construc. Co., dev.	213726	1938	
2000 Conn. Ave., NW		Apts.	Alvin Aubinoe + Harry L. Edwards, archs. (Harvey Warwick, assoc.) Cafritz Construc. Co.	192104	1936	
2100 Conn. Ave., NW		Apts.	Joseph Abel, arch. Chas. Oshinskey, dev.		1941	
2929 Conn. Ave., NW		Apts.	Joseph Abel, arch. H.K. Jawish + P. Townsend, devs.	195436	1936	
3133 Conn. Ave., NW	The Kennedy-Warren	Apt.-Hotel	Joseph Younger, arch. Henry Warren, Inc., dev.	140167	1932	
3726 Conn. Ave., NW	Sedgwick Gardens	Apts.	Mihran Mesrobian, arch. Max Gorin, dev.	146687	1932	

103

RESIDENTIAL	ADDRESS	NAME OF STRUCTURE	USE	ARCHITECT/ DEVELOPER	BUILDING PERMIT NO.	YEAR OF CONSTR.
	4607 Conn. Ave., NW	The Chesapeake	Apts.	M.G. Lepley, arch. Gorin + Horning, devs.	243385	1941
	4801 Conn. Ave., NW		Apts.	Joseph Abel + David L. Stern, arch. Alvin Aubinoe, dev.	217990	1938
	5429 Conn. Ave., NW	The Roberta	Apts.	Sidney Poretsky, arch. Harry Poretsky, dev.	236996	1940
	215 Constitution Ave., NE	The Congressional	Apts.	Alvin Aubinoe, arch. Alvin Aubinoe, dev.	226821	1939
	2803 Cortland Pl., NW		Garden Apts.	G.T. Santmyers, arch. Cortland Construc. Co., dev.	223612	1939
	3806-3822 Davis Pl., NW also 2514-2518 Tunlaw Rd., NW 2517-2519 39th St., NW		Garden Apts.	G.T. Santmyers, arch. Morris Silver, dev.	231295	1940
	3901-3905 Davis Pl., NW	Monte Vista	Garden Apts.	G.T. Santmyers, arch. Morris Silver, dev.	215166	1938
	4031 Davis Pl., NW		Garden Apts.	Dana B. Johannes, arch. H.E. Davis, dev.	217965	1938
	4115-4119 Davis Pl., NW (see listing for 42d St., NW)					
	2800-2824 Devonshire Pl., NW		Garden Apts.	G.T. Santmyers, arch. Cortland Contruc. Co., dev.	223612	1939
	35 E St., NW	Capitol Plaza Apts.	Apts.	arch. + year unknown		
	819 East Capitol St., SE	The Wiltshire	Apts.	L. White, arch. Harry Poretsky, dev.	185020	1935 (addition)
	4120-4124 Edmunds St., NW (see listing for 42d St., NW)					
	1900 F St., NW	Park Central (Mabel Nelson Thurston Hall: GWU dormitory)	Apt.-Hotel (now used as dormitory)	Harvey Warwick, arch. Cafritz Construc. Co., dev.	119865	1928
	2000 F St., NW	The Empire	Apts.	Harry L. Edwards, arch. Cafritz Construc. Co., dev.	222469	1939
	1325 Fort Stevens Dr., NW		Garden Apts.	Sam Novak, arch. Jos. A. Katz, dev.	221725	1939
	1329-1337 Ft. Stevens Dr., NW	Garden Manor	Garden Apts.	G.T. Santmyers, arch. Nalpak Realty Co., dev.	247449	1941
	1362 Fort Stevens Dr., NW		Garden Apts.	G.T. Santmyers, arch. Louis Luria, dev.	233754	1940
	1370-1372 Ft. Stevens Dr., NW	The Glade	Garden Apts.	G.T. Santmyers, arch. Nalpak Realty Co., dev.	223029	1939
	1376 Ft. Stevens Dr., NW		Garden Apts.	G.T. Santmyers, arch. Morris Lenkins Construc. Co., dev.	218861	1938
	1380 Ft. Stevens Dr., NW		Garden Apts.	G.T. Santmyers, arch. David L. Stern Construc. Co., dev.	216823	1938
	2301 Foxhall Rd., NW	"Cafritz Mansion"	Private Residence	Alvin Aubinoe + Harry L. Edwards, arch. Cafritz Construc. Co., dev.	196434	1936
	315-325 Franklin St., NE	Panorama Courts	Garden Apts.	Sam Novak, arch. Kol Construc. Co., dev.	218691	1938
	1615-1625 Franklin St., NE		Apts.	J.P. Fitzsimmons, arch. Colby Bldg. Corp., dev.	241677	1941

ADDRESS	NAME OF STRUCTURE	USE	ARCHITECT/ DEVELOPER	BUILDING PERMIT NO.	YEAR OF CONSTR.
6817 Georgia Ave., NW	The Normandie	Apts.	G.T. Santmyers, arch. Webster Construc. Co., dev.	210188	1938
7436 Georgia Ave., NW	The Sheperd	Garden Apts.	G.T. Santmyers, arch. Zarin + Korman, dev.	188879	1936
7611, 7701 Georgia Ave., NW		Apts.	L.T. Rouleau, arch. Seaboard Realty Co., dev.	143616 + 146091	1931
2223 H St., NW	The Everglades	Apts. (now used as a GWU dormitory)	Joseph Abel, arch. Harry Bralove, dev.	226920	1939
1650 Harvard St., NW	Harvard Hall	Apts.	Louis Justement, arch. Wm. S. Phillips, dev.	119742	1928
1210-1240 Holbrook Terr., NE	Holbrook Terrace	Garden Apts.	G.T. Santmyers, arch. Hamilton Construc. Co., Dev.	225551	1939
2025 I St., NW	Parklane	Apts.	Harvey Warwick, arch. Cafritz Construc. Co., dev.	5832	1928
2212 I St., NW	Munson Hall	Apts. (now used as a GWU dormitory)	Robert O. Scholz, arch. Meadowbrook, Inc., dev.	205711	1938
2222 I St., NW	Milton Hall	Apts. (now used as a GWU dormitory)	Robert O. Scholz, arch. Meadowbrook, Inc., dev.	217339	1938
701 K St., NE		Apts.	G.T. Santmyers, arch. Annette Apts. Inc., dev.	241647	1941
2515 K St., NW	The Bader	Apts.	Louis de Ladurantage, arch. A. Jos. Howar, dev.	222934	1939
1915 Kalorama Rd., NW	Connecticut Gardens	Apts.	Harry Poretsky, arch. Harry Poretsky, dev.	223038	1939
4014 Kansas Ave., NW		Garden Apts.	arch. unknown Isadore Young, dev.	225689	1939
21 + 25 Kennedy St., NW		Apts.	J.P. Fitzsimmons, arch. Harry Gorin, dev.	237709 + 243860	1940/1941
1660 Lanier Pl., NW		Apts.	Harry L. Edwards, arch. Cafritz Construc. Co., dev.	231754	1940
6323 Luzon Ave., NW	The Luzon	Apts.	G.T. Santmyers, arch. Luzon Corp., dev.	211077	1938
6600 Luzon Ave., NW		Apts.	arch. + year unknown		
3725 Macomb St., NW	Macomb Gardens	Apts.	G.T. Santmyers, arch. Gelman Construc. Co., dev.	203427	1937
1314 Mass. Ave., NW	Cel-Mar Towers	Apts.	Jarrett G. White, arch. James Baird Co. Inc., bldr.	194674	1936
1700 Maryland Ave., NE		Garden Apts.	Dana B. Johannes, arch. Barkley Bros., dev.	250348	1942
1701 Mass. Ave., NW	The Bay State	Apts.	Robert O. Scholz, arch. Vermont Co., dev.	220113	1939
1727 Mass. Ave., NW	Winthrop House	Apts.	Alvin Aubinoe, arch. Dominion Investment Co., dev.	235082	1940
Minnesota Ave, Ridge Road + B St., SE	Greenway	Garden Apts./ Housing Project	Harry L. Edwards, arch. Cafritz Construc. Co., dev.	237601 + 242044	1940–1941
430 Missouri Ave., NW	Concord Manor	Apts.	G.T. Santmyers, arch. Harry Cohen, dev.	247562	1941
1417 N St., NW		Apts.	Frank Tomlinson, arch. Lee Properties, Inc., dev.	211527 + 137568	1930/1938
2911 Newark St., NW	The Macklin	Apts.	Mihran Mesrobian, arch. Frank Macklin, dev.	224825	1939

RESIDENTIAL	ADDRESS	NAME OF STRUCTURE	USE	ARCHITECT/ DEVELOPER	BUILDING PERMIT NO.	YEAR OF CONSTR.
	1731 New Hampshire Ave., NW	The Granite State	Apts.	J.P. Fitzsimmons, ach. Harriet Brodie, dev.	235256	1940
	5301 New Hampshire Ave., NW		Garden Apts.	Claude Norton, arch. J. Chas. Shapiro, dev.	221099	1939
	5210 N. Capitol St.		Garden Apts.	G.T. Santmyers, arch. D.J. Dunigan, dev.	241428	1941
	1445 Ogden St., NW	Ogden Gardens	Apts.	Alvin Aubinoe + Harry L. Edwards, arch. Cafritz Construc. Co., dev.	200232	1937
	1445 Otis Pl., NW	Otis Gardens	Apts.	Alvin Aubinoe + Harry L. Edwards, arch. Cafritz Construc. Co., dev.	201084	1937
	1610 Park Rd., NW	The Parkhill	Apts.	Sam Novak, arch. Parkhill Co., dev.	240231	1941
	1371 Peabody St., NW		Garden Apts.	G.T. Santmyers, arch. Nalpak Realty, dev.	231520	1940
	2150 Penn. Ave., NW	The Keystone (H.B. Burns Mem. Bldg.)	Apts. (now used as a GWU medical bldg.)	Robert O. Scholz, arch. Baer + Scholz, dev.	140231	1931
	2801 Penn. Ave., SE		Garden Apts.	G.T. Santmyers, arch. Stearns-Mishkin Construc. Co., dev.	204505	1937
	2811 Penn. Ave., SE		Garden Apts.	Dana B. Johannes, arch. David M. Nolan, dev.	248522	1941
	3304 Penn. Ave., SE	Mount Dome	Garden Apts. + Stores	Bryan J. Connor, arch. Louis Brooks, dev.	226592	1939
	3984-3986 Penn. Ave., SE	Ave Manor	Garden Apts.	G.T. Santmyers, arch. B + M Construc. Co., dev.	255014	1942
	1732 Portal Drive, NW		Single-Family House	Bernard Lyon Frishman Assoc., arch. Barney Kraft, bldr.	291086	1946–7
	1901-09 Q St., NW	The Moorings	Apts. (now used as offices)	Horace Peaslee, arch. Mrs. J.R. Williams, dev.	8488	1927
	2511 Q St., NW	Rock Creek Gardens West	Apts.	Jos. J. Maggenti, arch. Jerry Maiatico, dev.	222570	1939
	1727 R St., NW		Apts.	William Barrington, arch. Home Construc. Co., dev.	224299	1939
	3210 Reservoir St., NW		Single-Family House	Theodore Dominick, arch. Alexander Hawes, dev.		1937
	200-210 Rhode Island Ave., NE	The Metropolitan	Apts.	G.T. Santmyers, arch. Kay Construc. Co., dev.	188258	1936
	230 Rhode Island Ave., NE	Rhode Island Gardens	Apts.	Harvey P. Baxter, arch. Monroe + Hugh Warren, devs.	142801	1931
	1 Scott Circle, NW	The General Scott	Apts.	Robert O. Scholz, arch. Robert O. Scholz, dev.	239352	1940
	1401 Sheridan St., NW	The Sheridan	Apts.	Bryan J. Connor, arch. Banks + Lee, dev.	223323	1939
	1400 Somerset Pl., NW		Apts.	Byran J. Connor, arch. Banks + Lee, dev.	223806	1939
	3828 S. Capitol St., SE		Garden Apts.	G.T. Santmyers, arch. S + R. Inc., dev.	262123	1943
	2514-2518 Tunlaw Rd., NW (see listing for Davis Pl.)					
	2915 University Terr., NW		Single-Family House	Howard D. Woodson, arch. Dr. Ethel L. Nixon-Mounsey, dev.	320176	1949

ADDRESS	NAME OF STRUCTURE	USE	ARCHITECT/ DEVELOPER	BUILDING PERMIT NO.	YEAR OF CONSTR.
1400 Van Buren St., NW		Garden Apts.	arch. + year unknown		
1301 Vermont Ave., NW	The Eddystone	Apts.	Robert O. Scholz, arch. Vermont Co., dev.	199717	1937
2121 Virginia Ave., NW	The Governor Shepherd	Apts. + Stores	Joseph Abel, arch. John J. McInerney, dev.	216080	1938
4101-4121 W St., NW (see listing for 42d St)					
2911 W St., SE		Single-Family House	John Jos. Earley, arch. Dr. M.S. Fealty, dev.	180984	1935
301-305 Whittier St., NW also 300-304 Aspen St., NW 6718-6722 3d St., NW	Whittier Gardens	Garden Apts.	G.T. Santmyers, arch. Ida Baylin, dev.	226673	1939
2700-2720 Wisconsin Ave., NW (see related styles)					
3130 Wisconsin Ave., NW	The Chancery	Apts.	M.G. Lepley, arch. Jerry Maiatico, dev.	245590	1941
2800 Woodley Rd., NW		Apts.	G.T. Santmyers, arch. L + S Construc. Co., dev.	241426	1941
1935 3d St., NE		Garden Apts.	G.T. Santmyers, arch. Harry Kay, dev.	229704	1940
6718-6722 3d St., NW (see listing for Whittier St.)					
5611 5th St., NW		Garden Apts.	G.T. Santmyers, arch. M. Platshon, dev.	191976	1936
4021 9th St., NW	Taylor Towers	Apts.	G.T. Santmyers, arch. Henry Oxenberg, dev.	220941	1939
317 10th St., NE		Apts.	G.T. Santmyers, arch.		1928
6000-6050 13th Pl., NW	Fort View Apts.	Garden Apts.	G.T. Santmyers, arch. Fort View Apts., dev.	219338	1939
5807-5825 14th St., NW		Garden Apts.	G.T. Santmyers, arch. Brown Bros. Corp., dev.	218489	1938
5915-5925 14th St., NW		Garden Apts.	G.T. Santmyers, arch. Louis Luria + Herman Shapiro, devs.	230419	1940
6101-6121 14th St., NW		Single-Family Houses (semi-detached)	Harry Sternfeld, arch. Frank Koplin, dev.	178304	1935
6437 14th St., NW		Garden Apts.	G.T. Santmyers, arch. S. Freedman, dev.	236893	1940
2325-31 15th St., NW	Garden Towers	Garden Apts.	arch. + year unknown probably Santmyers		
2407 15th St., NW (see related styles)					
2801 15th St., NW		Apts.	Edmund W. Dreyfuss, arch. Zellan Construc. Co., dev.	245612	1941
1112 16th St., NW	Pall Mall Apts.	Apts.	Robert O. Scholz, arch. David A. Baer, dev.	229507	1940
1530 16th St., NW	High Towers	Apts.	Alvin Aubinoe, arch. Cafritz Construc. Co., dev.		1938
1901 16th St., NW	The Anchor	Apts.	R.C. Archer, Jr., arch. Albert Dade, dev.	173916	1934
1926 16th St., NW		Apts.	arch. + year unknown		

RESIDENTIAL	ADDRESS	NAME OF STRUCTURE	USE	ARCHITECT/ DEVELOPER	BUILDING PERMIT NO.	YEAR OF CONSTR.
	2120 16th St., NW (see related styles)					
	2440 16th St., NW	Park Tower	Apts.	William Harris, arch. Goldsmith + Keller, devs.	117740	1928
	2480 16th St., NW	Dorchester House	Apts.	Francis Koenig, arch. Gustave Ring, dev.		1941
	2601 16th St., NW	Meridian Hill Hall	Hotel/Dormitory	Louis Justement, arch. Defense Homes Corp., dev.	250075	1942
	2651 16th St., NW	The Century	Apts.	Louis J. Rouleau, arch. White House Realty, dev.	197605	1936
	3150 16th St., NW		Apts.	arch. + year unknown		
	3200 16th St., NW	The Majestic	Apts.	Alvin Aubinoe + Harry L. Edwards, archs. Cafritz Construc. Co., dev.	202089	1937
	3355 16th St., NW	The Yorkshire	Apts.	G.T. Santmyers, arch. Yorkshire Corp., dev.	245935	1941
	1815 17th St., NW (see related styles)					
	2901 18th St., NW	Park Crescent	Apts.	Alvin Aubinoe + Harry L. Edwards, arch. Cafritz Construc. Co., dev.	206089	1937
	601 19th St., NW ⓓ	The Townhouse	Apts. + Stores	Harvey Baxter, arch. L.E. Breuninger + Sons, dev.	212689	1938
	1020 19th St., NW ⓓ	The Gwenwood	Apts.	Harry L. Edwards, arch. Cafritz Construc. Co., dev.	219284	1938
	21st + G St., NE	Langston Dwellings	Housing Project	Hilyard Robinson, arch.		1935–36
	515 22d St., NW	Park Manor	Apts.	Raymond G. Moore, arch. Park Manor, Inc., dev.	239012	1940
	2745 29th St., NW	The Delano	Apts.	G.T. Santmyers, arch. Brown Bros. Corp., dev.	243555	1941
	1735 33d Pl., SE		Garden Apts.	G.T. Santmyers, arch. Gerald Oxenberg, dev.	233385	1940
	3415 36th St., NW		Single-Family House	Waldron Faulkner, arch.		1937
	2517-2519 39th St., NW (see listing for Davis Pl.)					
	2201-2205 42d St., NW also 4101-4121 W St., NW 2300-2308 Benton St., NW	Park Crest Gardens	Garden Apts.	G.T. Santmyers, arch. Maurice Korman, dev.	243565	1941
	2615-2619 42d St., NW also 4115-4119 Davis Pl., NW 4120-4124 Edmunds St., NW	Park View Terrace	Garden Apts.	G.T. Santmyers, arch. Maurice Korman, dev.	222250	1939
Buildings in Montgomery County, Md.—listed alphabetically by streets	8700-8722 Colesville Rd., Silver Spring, Md.	Montgomery Arms	Garden Apts.	arch. + year unknown		
	9900 Colesville Rd., Silver Spring, Md.	Polychrome House #1	Single-Family House	John Joseph Earley + J.R. Kennedy, archs.		1934
	9904 Colesville Rd., Silver Spring, Md.		Single-Family House	J.J. Earley		1935
	7410 Connecticut Ave., Chevy Chase, Md.		Single-Family House	Mihran Mesrobian, arch.		1941

ADDRESS	NAME OF STRUCTURE	USE	ARCHITECT/ DEVELOPER	BUILDING PERMIT NO.	YEAR OF CONSTR.	RESIDENTIAL
5150 Mass. Ave., Bethesda, Md.		Single-Family House	architect + year unknown			
9919, 9923, 9925 Sutherland Rd., Silver Spring, Md.		Single-Family Houses	J.J. Earley, arch.		1935	
6306 Wisconsin Ave., Chevy Chase, Md.		Single-Family House	arch. & year unknown			
5516 Auth Rd., Camp Springs, Md.		Single-Family House	Design (#6692) by Garlinghouse Plan Service (Topeka, Kan.)		1948	Buildings in Prince George's County, Md.—listed by alphabetical, followed by numerical, streets
6905 Baltimore Ave., College Park, Md.		Single-Family House	arch. + year unknown			
3900 Hamilton St., Hyattsville, Md.	Prince George's Apts.	Garden Apts.	Eugene B. Roberts, dev.			
4112, 4114, 4206 Queensbury Rd., Riverdale, Md.		Garden Apts.	probably Santmyers			
6911 21st Ave., Hyattsville, Md.		Single-Family House	Design (#6692) by Garlinghouse Plan Service (Topeka, Kans.) Parris Rizzo, bldr.		1948	
6202 42d Ave., Riverdale, Md.		Garden Apts.	probably Santmyers			
1537-1545 Key Blvd., Arlington, Va.		Garden Apts.	Albert D. Lueders, arch. Clyde Dasher, dev.		1941	Buildings in Arlington County, Va.
1925–27 Calvert St.		Garden Apts.	arch. + year unknown			
1233 N. Court House Rd., Arlington, Va.		Garden Apts.	Mihran Mesrobian, arch. F + W Construc. Co., dev.		1940	
2416-2424 N. 16th St., Arlington, Va.		Garden Apts.	arch. + year unknown			
4012 25th Rd., Arlington, Va.		Single-Family House	John Sullivan Kennedy, arch. & bldr.		1940	
3301 Cameron Mills, Rd., Alexandria, Md.		Single-Family House	arch. + year unknown			Buildings in Alexandria, Va.
412, 414, 420, 422 East Glendale Ave., Alexandria, Va.		Garden Apts.	arch. + year unknown			

ADDRESS	NAME OF STRUCTURE	USE	ARCHITECT/ DEVELOPER	BUILDING PERMIT NO.	YEAR OF CONSTR.	COMMERCIAL
911 Bladensburg Rd., NE	Sears Roebuck + Co.	Dept. Store	Nimmons, Carr + Wright	122584	1929	Buildings in District of Columbia— listed by alphabetical, followed by numerical, streets
2606 Conn. Ave., NW	Arbaugh's	Restaurant			ca. 1938	
3419 Conn. Ave., NW	Roma	Restaurant	A.S.J. Atkinson, arch. Chas. G. Kennon, Inc., bldr.	191082	1936	
3400-Block, Conn. Ave., NW		Storefronts				
3524 Conn. Ave., NW	Yenching Palace	Restaurant	R.C. Archer, Jr., arch. Anna Sabin + Henry Crossen, devs.	278948	1945	
4433-65 Conn. Ave., NW		Neighborhood Shopping Center	Chevy Chase Park + Shop Stores	217222	1938	
4483 Conn. Ave., NW	Hahn Shoes	Store	William M. Denton, Jr., arch.	219206	1938	
1013 E St., NW	M.E. Swing, Inc.	Retail Store	(Deco Interior)			
2125 E St., NW	Peoples Drug	Store	William E.C. Barrington, arch. Banks + Lee, bldrs.	226085	1939	

109

ADDRESS	NAME OF STRUCTURE	USE	ARCHITECT/ DEVELOPER	BUILDING PERMIT NO.	YEAR OF CONSTR.
1211 F St., NW	Wilbur-Rogers, Inc. (now Simco shoes)	Store	Solomon Kaplan, arch. Wilbur-Rogers, Inc., dev.	164316	1931
1230 F St., NW	Remington-Rand Bldg. (now Deyoung Shoes)	Offices/Stores/ Restaurant	Holabird + Root, archs.		1935
1300 F St., NWⒹ	Brownley's Bldg. (#1)	Stores + Restaurant	Porter + Lockie, archs.	153871	1932
1305 F St., NWⒹ	Massey Shoes	Store	Chas. S. Telchin, archs. Cladny Construc. Co., dev.	235316	1940
1309 F St., NW	Brownley's Bldg. (#2)	Offices + Store	Porter + Lockie, archs.	155233	1932
1326 Florida Ave., NW	Manhattan Co.	Laundry	A.M. Pringle + Bedford Brown IV. archs. Pringle Construc. Co., dev.	197250	1936
1112 G St., NWⒹ	Neisner's	Dept. Store			1948
1239 G St., NW	Jordan Foundation Music Store	Store	Donald Johnson, arch. Chas. H. Tompkins, dev.	291131	1946
1407 G St., NW	Liberty Bldg. Assoc.	Bank	Porter + Lockie, archs.	293968	1947
5915 Georgia Ave., NW	Seven Seas	Restaurant	Wm. Russell Wheeler, arch. A. Weiss, bldr.	213024	ca. 1938
Georgia Ave. + Sheridan St., NW		Shopping Center	John Eberson, arch. Kass Realty, Inc., dev.	192689 + 193773	1937
627 H St., NW	China Doll	Restaurant	arch. + year unknown		
1230 H St., NW	White Tower	Restaurant	arch. + year unknown		
1217-19 K St., NWⒹ	National Cash Register	Offices	E. Burton Corning, arch. Geo. C. Martin, bldr.	212173	1938
1401 K St., NW	Tower Bldg.	Office Bldg.	Robert F. Beresford, arch. William L. Browning, dev.	9449	1928
1625 K St., NW	Commonwealth Bldg.	Office Bldg.	Harvey Warwick, arch. Alvin Aubinoe, dev.	246530	1941
1627 K St., NWⒹ	Heurich Bldg.	Office Bldg.	Frank Russell White, arch. Anita Eckles + Karia King, devs.	193009	1936
112 Kennedy St., NW		Vitrolite Facade		A-17938	1951?
116 Kennedy St., NW		Store	Arthur P. Starr, arch. David L. Stern/Central Realty Co., dev.	199792	1937
131 M St., NE	Woodward + Lothrop Warehouse	Warehouse	Abbot, Merkt + Co. (NY), archs.	215215	1938
3111 M St., NW	F.W. Woolworth + Co.	Dept. Store	F.W. Woolworth Co., arch. H. Kaplan Co., dev.	233480	1940
3256 M St., NW	W.H. Brewton + Sons	Store	Dana B. Johannes, arch. Colonial Bldrs. Inc., dev.	209702 + 211909	1938
2022 Martin Luther King Ave., SE (orig. Nichols Ave.)		Beauty Parlor	W. Ellis Groben, arch. G.W. Scherman, dev.	299322	1947
2107 Martin Luther King Ave., SE		Store	Frank B. Proctor, arch. Jane Corbin, dev.	220690	1939
3016 Martin Luther King Ave., SE		Store/Laundry	Johannes + Murray, arch. Congress Bldg. Co., dev.	298338	1947
317 Mass. Ave., NEⒹ	Bosley Dog + Cat Hospital	Animal Hospital	Ernest T. Davis, arch. Milton O. Bosley, dev.	207835	1937

ADDRESS	NAME OF STRUCTURE	USE	ARCHITECT/ DEVELOPER	BUILDING PERMIT NO.	YEAR OF CONSTR.
2412 Minn. Ave., SE		Offices + Store	Frank Martinelli, arch. A.G. Carozza, dev.	317237	1949
3932 Minn. Ave., NE	F.W. Woolworth + Co.	Dept. Store	Frank Beatty, arch. Fred Kogod, dev.	300377 + 308205	1947
1110 New York Ave., NW	Greyhound Terminal	Bus Station	Wischmeyer, Arrasmith + Elswick, archs. (Louisville, Ky.)	223145	1939
1401 New York Ave., NE	Hecht Company Warehouse	Warehouse	Abbot, Merkt + Co. (N.Y.), archs.	193803	1937
666 Penn Ave., SE	S.S. Kresge	Dept. Store	S.S. Kresge Co., arch. Lee T. Turner, bldg.	198203	1936
2324 Penn. Ave., SE	Morton's	Dept. Store	Evan J. Connor, arch. Harry Dobkin, dev.	217342	1938
4001-4005 S. Capitol St., SW	F.W. Woolworth + Co.	Dept. Store	Frank Beatty, arch. Fred Kogod, dev.	294255	1947
1331 U St., NW		Warehouse	A.S.J. Atkinson, arch. Glassman + Ostrow, dev.	198628	1937
1000 Vermont Ave., NW	Wire Building	Office Bldg.	Alvin Aubinoe, arch. Preston + Raymond Wire, dev.	314278	1948
4500 Wisconsin Ave., NW	Sears Roebuck + Co.	Dept. Store	John Stokes Redden, arch.	238208	1940
5210 Wisconsin Ave., NW	Pepco Substation	Power Station	Company arch.	229744	1940
5248 Wisconsin Ave., NW ⓓ	Tolman Laundry	Laundry	The Austin Company, arch. + bldr.	127919	1929
5324 Wisconsin Ave., NW ⓓ	Silver Fox Restaurant	Restaurant	A.R. Clas, arch. Nevair Corp., dev.	284206	1946
5422 1st Pl., NW	Quality Valet Service	Store/Laundry	Sign by Edward Hurman, Alice G. Chumbris, dev.	207125	1937?
526 1st St., NW	Salvation Army	Stores + Dwellings	Col. P.M. Anderson, arch. Schneider + Spliedt Co., bldrs.	175531	1934
418 7th St., NW	Lansburgh's	Dept. Store	Porter + Lockie, archs.		1940
434 7th St., NW	S.S. Kresge	Dept. Store	arch. unknown		1934
7th + K St., NW	Hahn's Shoes	Store	Porter + Lockie, archs.		1938
422 10th St., NW ⓓ	Star Parking Plaza	Parking Garage	Porter + Lockie, archs. J.J. Earley, Assoc. Evening Star Newspaper Co., dev.	225767	1940
512 10th St., NW	Pepco Substation	Power Station (now used by Univ. of Southern California)	John Loehler, arch.		ca. 1950
3726 10th St., NE	Atlantic Electric Supply Corp.	Store	William E.C. Barrington, arch. Home Construc. Co., dev.	215693	1938
3730-3746 10th St., NE		Shopping Center	Hyman Cunin, arch. Home Construc. Co., dev.	213520	1938
501 11th St., NW	Whitlow's	Restaurant			
517 11th St., SE	Chambers Funeral Home	Mortuary	Leroy H. Harris, arch. W.W. Chambers, dev.	159275	1932
516 12th St., NW		Shop	Jos. Baumer, arch. Geo. Miller, dev.	162791	1933
730 12th St., NW	C + P Telephone Co. Bldg.	Office Bldg.	Ralph T. Walker, arch.		1928
734 15th St., NW	Walker Bldg.	Office Bldg.	Porter + Lockie, archs. (J.J. Earley, Assoc.) W.M. Walker, dev.	198581	1937

111

COMMERCIAL	ADDRESS	NAME OF STRUCTURE	USE	ARCHITECT/ DEVELOPER	BUILDING PERMIT NO.	YEAR OF CONSTR.
	1012 20th St., NW	Post Building	Offices	Louis Justement, arch. Jos. Nebel, bldr.	284093	1946
	2001 20th St., NW		Offices	arch. + year unknown		
Buildings in Montgomery County, Md.	6950-7000 Carroll Ave., Takoma Park, Md.		Office Bldg.	arch. + year unknown		
	7001 Carroll Ave., Takoma Park, Md.		Store	arch. + year unknown		
	8656 Colesville Rd., Silver Spring, Md.	J.C. Penney	Dept. Store	arch. + year unknown		
	4 Courthouse Sq., Rockville, Md.	Farmers Banking + Trust	Bank	Tilghman-Moyer Co., arch. (Allentown, Pa.)		1930
	1110 East-West Hwy., Silver Spring, Md.	Coca Cola Bottling Plant	Industrial Bldg.	arch. unknown		1941
	1201 East-West Hwy., Silver Spring, Md.	Canada Dry Bottling Plant	Industrial Bldg.	Walter Monroe Cory, arch. (NY)		1946
	Fenton St. + Ellsworth Drive, Silver Spring, Md.	Hecht Co.	Dept. Store	arch. + year unknown		
	7900-7910 Georgia Ave., Silver Spring, Md.		Storefronts	arch. + year unknown		
	8012 Georgia Ave., Silver Spring, Md.	Crisfield's	Restaurant	Sign by Jack Stone Co.		ca. 1945
	8516 Georgia Ave., Silver Spring, Md.	Tastee Diner	Diner	arch. unknown		1946
	8555 Georgia Ave., Silver Spring, Md.		Shopping Center	John Eberson, arch. Alexander Realty Co., dev.		1938
	8621 Georgia Ave., Silver Spring, Md.		Office Bldg.	arch. + year unknown		
	11400-Block Georgia Ave., Wheaton, Md.	Wheaton Shopping Center	Shopping Center	arch. + year unknown		
	2408 University Blvd., Wheaton, Md.	Short Stop Diner	Diner	arch. + year unknown		
	University Blvd., Wheaton, Md.	WTOP Transmitter	Radio Station	E. Burton Corning, arch. Geo. C. Martin, bldr.		1939
	7731 Woodmont Ave., Bethesda, Md.	Tastee Diner	Diner (altered)	arch. + year unknown		
Buildings in Prince George's County, Md.	5100-Block Baltimore Ave., Hyattsville, Md.	Magruder Flatiron Bldg.	Offices + Stores	Paul Kea, arch.		
	5600 Baltimore Ave., Hyattsville, Md.	Lustine Oldsmobile	Auto Dealer			
	7215 Baltimore Ave., College Park, Md.		Streamlined Bldg.	arch. + year unknown		
	5400 block Queen's Chapel Rd., 3100 block Hamilton St., Hyattsville, Md.	Queen's Chapel Shopping Center	Shopping Center	arch. + year unknown		
	118 Washington Blvd., Laurel, Md.	Tastee Diner		arch. + year unknown		

ADDRESS	NAME OF STRUCTURE	USE	ARCHITECT/ DEVELOPER	BUILDING PERMIT NO.	YEAR OF CONSTR.	COMMERCIAL
2811 Columbia, Pike, Arlington, Va.		Shopping Center	Cladny Construc. Co. (?)			**Buildings in Arlington County, Va.**
3100 Lee Hwy., Arlington, Va.	National Pawnbrokers	Store	arch. unknown	35996	1939	
4001 Lee Hwy., Arlington, Va.	Progressive Cleaners	Laundry	arch. unknown		ca. 1940	
9715 Lee Hwy., Arlington, Va.	Bob's Diner	Diner	arch. + year unknown			
1101 N. Highland St., Arlington, Va.	Old Dominion Bldg.	Office Bldg.	Muhleman + Kayhoe, bldrs.		ca. 1940	
1130 N. Highland St., Arlington, Va. Ⓓ		Medical Bldg.	Raymond G. Moore, arch. Muhleman + Kayhoe, bldrs.		1940	
3100 Washington Blvd., Arlington, Va.		Store	Muhleman + Kayhoe, bldrs.		ca. 1945	
5800 block Washington Blvd., Arlington, Va.	Westover Shopping Center	Shopping Center (altered)	E.L. Daniels, bldr.	20765	1947	
2825 Wilson Blvd., Arlington, Va.		Auto Dealer	Lyon Inc., bldr.		ca. 1939	
3028 Wilson Blvd., Arlington, Va.	The Quality Shop	Store	arch. unknown	22889	1935	
3101 Wilson Blvd., Arlington, Va.	Hahn Shoes	Store	Raymond G. Moore, arch.		1941	
3910 Wilson Blvd., Arlington, Va.		Auto Dealer	J. Raymond Mims, arch. Roystone, Grimm + Sammons, bldrs.		ca. 1948	
1321, 1406, 1423, 1509 E. Alexandria Ave., Alexandria, Va.		Commercial Buildings	arch. + year unknown			**Buildings in Alexandria, Va.**
901 King St., Alexandria, Va.	Shaffer Florists	Store	arch. + year unknown			
911 King St., Alexandria, Va.	New Majestic Restaurant	Restaurant	arch. + year unknown			
1101 King St., Alexandria, Va. Ⓓ	Aero Chevrolet	Auto Dealer	arch. + year unknown			
1316 Mt. Vernon Ave., Alexandria, Va.	Phone Co. Bldg.	Offices	arch. unknown			
1509-1517 Mt. Vernon Ave., Alexandria, Va.		Retail Stores	arch. + year unknown			
1800 Mt. Vernon Ave., Alexandria, Va.		Garage	arch. + year unknown			
2213 Mt. Vernon Ave., Alexandria, Va.		Retail Store	arch. + year unknown			
2413 Mt. Vernon Ave., Alexandria, Va.		Retail Store	arch. + year unknown			
2423-2429 Mt. Vernon Ave., Alexandria, Va.		Retail Stores	arch. + year unknown			
3800 block Mt. Vernon Ave., Alexandria, Va.	Arlandria Shopping Center	Shopping Center	arch. + year unknown			
300 N. Henry St., Alexandria, Va.		Store	arch. + year unknown			
600 N. Henry St., Alexandria, Va.		Offices	arch. + year unknown			

COMMERCIAL	ADDRESS	NAME OF STRUCTURE	USE	ARCHITECT/ DEVELOPER	BUILDING PERMIT NO.	YEAR OF CONSTR.
Building in Fairfax County, Va.	10536 Lee Hwy.	Tastee Diner	Diner	arch. + year unknown		

RECREATIONAL	ADDRESS	NAME OF STRUCTURE	USE	ARCHITECT/ DEVELOPER	BUILDING PERMIT NO.	YEAR OF CONSTR.
Buildings in District of Columbia— listed by alphabetical, followed by numerical, streets	2834 Ala. Ave., SE	Naylor	Movie Theater (closed)	John J. Zink, arch. Kogod-Burka, dev.		1945
	21 Atlantic Ave., SW	Atlantic	Movie Theater (closed)	John Eberson, arch. Fairlawn Amusement Co., dev.	274905	1944
	2501 Benning Rd., NE	Langston	Movie Theater (closed)	John J. Zink, arch. Langston Theater Corp., dev.	275782	1945
	1230 C St., NE	Home Theater	Movie Theater (closed)	arch. + year unknown		
	3426 Conn. Ave., NW	Uptown	Movie Theater	John J. Zink, arch.	189930	1936
	6225 Georgia Ave., NW	Sheridan	Movie Theater (closed)	John Eberson, arch. Kass Realty, Inc., dev.	192689	1937
	1415 Good Hope Rd., SEⒹ	Anacostia	Movie Theater	John Eberson, arch. Fairlawn Amusement Co.	280819	1947
	1329-31 H St., NE	Atlas	Movie Theater (closed)	John J. Zink, arch. Kogod-Burka, dev.	210377	1939
	1661 Kalorama Rd., NW	"America on Wheels"	Roller Skating Rink	Frank Grad + Sons, arch. Chas. K. Tompkins, bldr.		1946
	4859 MacArthur Blvd., NW	MacArthur	Movie Theater	John J. Zink, arch. K-B Amusement Co., dev.	279547	1946
	4813 Mass. Ave., NWⒹ	Apex	Movie Theater	John J. Zink, arch.		1940
	3950 Minn. Ave., NE	Senator	Movie Theater	John J. Zink, arch.	247149	1942
	644 Penn. Ave., SE	Penn	Movie Theater (closed)	John Eberson, arch. Stanley Co. of America, dev.	183590	1935
	2105 Penn. Ave., NW	Circle	Movie Theater	Luther R. Ray, arch. Circle Amusement, Co., dev.	153575	1932–35
	2533 Penn. Ave., SE	Highland	Movie Theater (closed)	John Eberson, arch. Fairlawn Amusement Co., dev.	234272	1940
	2324 Wisconsin Ave., NWⒹ	Calvert	Movie Theater	John Eberson, arch. Warner Bros., dev.		1937
	3601 12th St., NE	Newton	Movie Theater	John J. Zink, arch. Jesse Sherwood, dev.	199763	1937
	501 13th St., NW	Warner	Theater (Deco Ticket Booth)	C. Howard Crane, arch.	10592	1924–ca. 1950 Adapt.
	734 14th St., NWⒹ	Trans-Lux	Movie Theater	Thomas Lamb, arch. Trans-Lux Corp., dev.	193979	1936
	3030 14th St., NWⒹ	Savoy	Movie Theater	Edmund Dreyfuss, arch. (?) Stanley Co. of America	249795	ca. 1941
	517-23 15th St., NEⒹ	Beverly	Movie Theater	John Eberson, arch. Kass Realty, dev.	215212	1938
Buildings in Montgomery County, Md.	120 Commerce Lane, Rockville, Md.Ⓓ	Milo	Movie Theater	John J. Zink, arch. Sidney Lust, dev.		1936
	8619 Colesville Rd., Silver Spring, Md.	Silver	Movie Theater	John Eberson, arch. Alexander Realty Co., dev.		1938
	8725 Flower Ave., Silver Spring, Md.	Flower	Movie Theater	John J. Zink, arch.		1950
	MacArthur Blvd., Glen Echo, Md.	Glen Echo Park	Amusement Park (partially closed)	Alexander, Becker + Schoeppe, archs. (Philadelphia)		1931–39
	7719 Wisconsin Ave., Bethesda, Md.	Bethesda	Movie Theater	John Eberson, arch. Sidney Lust, dev.		1938

ADDRESS	NAME OF STRUCTURE	USE	ARCHITECT/ DEVELOPER	BUILDING PERMIT NO.	YEAR OF CONSTR.	RECREATIONAL
5612 Baltimore Blvd., Hyattsville, Md.Ⓓ	Hyattsville	Movie Theater	John Eberson, arch. Globe Amusement Co., dev.		1939	**Buildings in Prince George's County, Md.**
5445 Landover Rd., Cheverly, Md.	Cheverly	Movie Theater	John Eberson, arch.		1947	
4907 Marlboro Pike, Prince George's County	Coral	Movie Theater (closed)	John Eberson, arch. Kaufman + Steiner, devs.		1948	
2211 Varnum St., Mt. Ranier, Md.	Kaywood	Movie theater (closed)	Frank G. Ackerman, arch. A.S. Kay, dev.		1945	
1730 Wilson Blvd., Arlington, Va.	Wilson	Movie theater	Crown Dev't Corp. arch. unknown		1936	**Building in Arlington County, Va.**
1723 King St., Alexandria, Va.Ⓓ	Reed	Movie Theater	John J. Zink, arch. Alexandria Amusement Co.	1169	1936	**Buildings in Alexandria, Va.**
807 N. St. Asaph St., Alexandria, Va.	"America on Wheels"	Roller Skating Rink	Frank Grad + Sons, arch. Chas. K. Thompkins, bldr.			
601 1st St., Alexandria, Va.Ⓓ	Virginia	Movie Theater	John Eberson, arch. Alexandria Amusement Co.	3748	1947	

ADDRESS	NAME OF STRUCTURE	USE	ARCHITECT/ DEVELOPER	BUILDING PERMIT NO.	YEAR OF CONSTR.	INSTITUTIONAL + PUBLIC
Calvert St., NW	Duke Ellington Memorial Bridge	Bridge	Paul P. Cret, arch. Leon Hermant, Sculptor		1935	**Buildings in District of Columbia— listed by alphabetical, followed by numerical, streets**
Connecticut Ave., NW	Klingle Valley Bridge	Bridge	Paul P. Cret, arch. Frank M. Masters, Assoc.		1931	
3430 Conn. Ave., NW	Cleveland Park Post Office	Post Office	C. Meigs, arch.	235652	1940	
Constitution Ave. between 6th + 7th Sts., NW	Federal Trade Commission	Federal Building	Bennett, Parsons + Frost, archs.		1937	
Constitution Ave. between 9th + 10th Sts., NW	Department of Justice	Federal Building	Zantzinger, Borie + Medary, archs. (Philadelphia) J. J. Earley, cons.		1935	
201 E. Capitol St., SE	Folger Shakespeare Library	Library	Paul P. Cret, arch. Alexander B. Trowbridge, cons.	130151	1932	
212 E. Capitol St., NE	Lutheran Church of the Reformation	Church	Porter + Lockie, archs.	168229	1934	
2001 E. Capitol St., NE	District of Columbia Armory	Armory	Nathan C. Wyeth, arch.		1941	
441 G St., NW	General Accounting Office	Federal Building	Gilbert Stanley Underwood, arch.		1949	
2013 G St., NW	Stuart Hall	GWU classrooms	Edwin Weine + R.D. Barnes, archs.	192973	1936	
2023 G St., NW	Lisner Hall	GWU classrooms	Waldron Faulkner, arch.	219742 + 219824	1939	
2029 G St., NW	Bell Hall	GWU classrooms	Waldron Faulkner, arch.	181447	1935	
300 Indiana Ave., NW	Municipal Center	D.C. Govt. Offices	Nathan C. Wyeth, arch.	224667	1941	
2d St. + Independence Ave., SE	Library of Congress Annex	Library	Pierson + Wilson, archs. Alexander Trowbridge, cons.		1939	
1851 9th St., NW	Odd Fellows Temple	Meeting Hall	Albert I. Cassell, arch.	149801	1932	

INSTITUTIONAL + PUBLIC	ADDRESS	NAME OF STRUCTURE	USE	ARCHITECT/ DEVELOPER	BUILDING PERMIT NO.	YEAR OF CONSTR.
	13th + C Sts., SW	Central Heating + Refrigeration Plant	Industrial Structure	Paul P. Cret, arch.		1933
	14th + Shepherd Sts., NE	Holy Name College	college/monastery	Chester Oakley, arch. Franciscan Friars, bldr.		1930
	2800 16th St., NW	Scottish Rite Temple	Private Institution	Porter, Lockie + Chatelain, archs.	219611	1939
	817 23d St., NW		GWU Building	arch. + year unknown		
	29th St., NW	West Heating Plant	Industrial Structure	Gilbert Stanley Underwood, arch. W.M. Foster, cons. arch. Fed. Works Admin.		1946
	31st + South Sts., NW		Power Plant	arch. + year unknown		
Buildings in Montgomery County, Md.	Carderock, Montgomery County	David W. Taylor Model Basin	Naval R + D Center	Ben Moreell, USN, arch. J.J. Earley, cons.		1939
	8901 Wisconsin Ave., Bethesda, Md.	U.S. Naval Medical Center	Hospital	F.W. Southworth, arch. Paul P. Cret, cons.		1940
	MacArthur Blvd., Bon Air Heights, Md.	Ruth Bldg.	Defense Mapping Agency Facility	arch. + year unknown		
Buildings in Prince George's County, Md.	Crescent Rd., Greenbelt, Md.	Greenbelt Center School	School	Douglas Ellington + Reginald D. Wadsworth, archs.		1936–37
	8950 Edmonston Rd., Greenbelt, Md.	Greenbelt Middle School	School	Douglas Ellington + Reginald D. Wadsworth, archs.		
Buildings in Alexandria, Va.	1319 King St., Alexandria, Va. Ⓓ	Virginia "ABC" Store	State Liquor Store	arch. unknown		1951
	Mt. Vernon Parkway, Alexandria, Va.	Washington National Airport	Airport	Public Buildings Admin. Howard Cheney, cons. arch.		1940
	1005 Mt. Vernon Ave., Alexandria, Va.	George Washington Jr. High School	School	Raymond V. Long, chief arch., Va. State School Div. Col. James Anderson, chief eng., Public Works Admin.		1935
	117 S. Washington St., Alexandria, Va.		Military Recruiting Offices	arch. unknown		1930

RELATED + TRANSITIONAL	ADDRESS	NAME OF STRUCTURE	USE	ARCHITECT/ DEVELOPER	BUILDING PERMIT NO.	YEAR OF CONSTR.
Special Listing: Little Tavern Shops	5100 Georgia Ave., NW			G. Bluenner, arch.	167392	1933
	2716 Good Hope Rd., SE			arch. + year unknown		
	718 H St., NE			G. Bluenner, arch.	183945	1935
	1110 H St., NW			Lee W. Luttrell	194523	1936
	3331 M St., NW			Lee W. Luttrell	187588	1936
	530 Morse St., NE			arch. + year unknown		
	3701 N.H. Ave., NW			George Locknane	118972	1928
	630 N. Capitol St.			G.E. Stone	140149	1931
	2537 Penn. Ave., SE			Chas. Zeller	311184	1948
	1301 Wisconsin Ave., NW			Frank B. Proctor	210221	1938
	8230 Georgia Ave., Silver Spring, Md.			arch. + year unknown		

ADDRESS	NAME OF STRUCTURE	USE	ARCHITECT/ DEVELOPER	BUILDING PERMIT NO.	YEAR OF CONSTR.	RELATED + TRANSITIONAL
11143 Viers Mill Rd., Wheaton, Md.			arch. + year unknown			
Wayne Ave. + Fenton, Silver Spring, Md.			arch. + year unknown			
8100 Wisconsin Ave., Bethesda, Md.			arch. + year unknown			
7413 Balt. Blvd., College Park, Md.			arch. + year unknown			
Washington Blvd., Laurel, Md.			arch. + year unknown			
3110 Lee Hwy., Arlington, Va.			arch. + year unknown			
3121 Wilson Blvd., Arlington, Va.			arch. unknown	2236	1939	
828 N. Washington St., Alexandria, VA.			arch. + year unknown			
4116-36 Arkansas Ave., NW		Houses (semi-detached)	Jos. Abel, arch. J.B. Tiffey, dev.	229400	1940	**Buildings in District of Columbia—** listed by alphabetical, followed by numerical, streets
C St. between 18th + 19th Sts., NW	Department of the Interior	Federal Building	Waddy B. Wood, arch.		1935	
2500 Calvert St., NW	Shoreham Hotel	Hotel	Jos. Abel, arch.	129956	1930	
4000 Cathedral Ave., NW	The Westchester	Apt.-Hotel	Harvey Warwick, arch. Westchester Devt. Corp.	131047	1930	
1346 Conn. Ave., NW	Dupont Circle Building	Hotel-Office Bldg.	Mihran Mesrobian, arch. Joseph J. Moebs, dev.		1931	
5500 block Conn. Ave., NW	Chevy Chase Arcade	Shopping Arcade	arch. unknown		ca. 1930	
2737 Devonshire Pl., NW	Woodley Park Towers	Apt. Bldg.	Louis T. Rouleau, arch. Ell + Kay Bldg. + Invest's	121086	1929	
929 E St., NW	Pepco Office Building	Office Bldg.	Waddy B. Wood, arch.	132639	1930	
2025 E St., NW	American Red Cross	Office Bldg.	Eggers + Higgins, archs.		1951–52	
45 E St., NW	Pepco Sub-Station	Power Station	John Loehler, arch.		ca. 1950's	
211 Elm St., NW	Carver Hall Howard Univ.	Dormitory	Hilyard Robinson, arch. Defense Homes Corp., dev.	252791	1942	
300 Independence Ave., SW	U.S. Dept. of Health + Human Services	Federal Building (orig. Fed. Security Agency)	Louis A. Simon, arch. Chas. Z. Klauder, cons.		1939	
1249 Irving St., NE		Single-Family House (International Style)	H.H. Mackey, arch. Jos. Hopkinson, bldr.	309656	1948	
51 Louisiana Ave., NW	Acacia Mutual Life Insur. Co.	Office Bldg.	Shreve, Lamb + Harmon (New York) archs.	184187	1935	
208 Mass. Ave., NE	Capitol Towers	Apt. Bldg.	Harvey Warwick, arch. Southern Constr. Co.	121735	1929	
1312-1320 New York Ave., NW ⑬	Capital Garage	Parking Garage	Arthur B. Heaton, arch.		1926	
N. Capitol St. + G St. Place, NE	GPO Warehouse	Warehouse	Victor Abel, arch.		1938	
1111 N. Capitol St., NE	Smithsonian Instit. Service Center	Warehouse				
1741 Rhode Island Ave., NW	Longfellow Bldg.	Office Bldg. (International Style)	William Lescaze, arch.		1940	

RELATED + TRANSITIONAL	ADDRESS	NAME OF STRUCTURE	USE	ARCHITECT/ DEVELOPER	BUILDING PERMIT NO.	YEAR OF CONSTR.
	2700 Wisconsin Ave., NW	Highview	Apt. Bldg.	Joseph Abel, arch. Edwin C. Shelton, dev.	244823	1941
	2702 Wisconsin Ave., NW	Sherry Hall	Apt. Bldg.	Joseph Abel, arch. Meyer Siegel, dev.	252281	1942
	2712 Wisconsin Ave., NW	Wisconsin House	Apt. Bldg.			
	2720 Wisconsin Ave., NW		Apt. Bldg.	Joseph Abel, arch. Henry K. Jawish, dev.	231404	1940
	300 6th St., NW®	Orienta Coffee (Browning + Baines, Inc.)	Light Industrial Bldg.	arch. + year unknown		
	417 9th St., SE	Southeast Hebrew Congregation	Synagogue	arch. unknown	298865	1949
	2244 10th St., NW	Pepco Sub-Station	Power Station	Arthur B. Heaton, arch.	132707	1930
	14th St. + Jackson, NE	Lucy Slowe School		Office of D.C. Municipal architect		1949
	920 15th St., NW	Southern Railway Building	Office Bldg.	Waddy B. Wood, arch.	118738	1928
	2407 15th St., NW		Apt. Bldg.	Joseph Abel, arch.		
	2120 16th St., NW	Washington House	Apt. Bldg.	Joseph Abel, arch. Sovereign Properties, dev.	236118	1940
	4606 16th St., NW	B'Nai Israel Congregation	Synagogue	Maurice Courland, (New York) arch.	287372	1946
	1815 17th St., NW	The Croydon	Apt. Bldg.	Joseph Abel, arch. John J. McInerney, dev.		1941
	3437-53 17th St., NW		Houses (semi-detached)	E. Burton Corning, arch. Preston E. Wire, dev.	213469	1938
Buildings in Montgomery County, Md.	Bethesda, Md.	Old N.I.H. Hospital	Hospital	G.S.A., arch. Vincent Blinsky, sculptor (elevator doors)		1948–1952
	8821 River Rd., Bethesda, Md.	Norwood School	School (originally residence)	arch. + year unknown		
	7700 Carroll Ave., Takoma Park, Md.	Sligo Seventh-Day Adventist Church	Church	J. Raymond Mims, arch. (Mims-Speake)		1944
	6124 MacArthur Blvd., Bon Air Heights, Md.	Bonfield's Texaco	Gas Station	arch. unknown		ca. 1928
Buildings in Prince George's County, Md.	Brentwood, Md.	Ft. Lincoln Cemetery—Community Mausoleum	Mausoleum	Harley, Ellington, Cowing + Sturton, arch. (Southfield, Mich.)		1948
	Greenbelt Rd., Greenbelt, Md.	Greenbelt Armory	Armory	Lawrence V. Sangston, arch.		1954
Buildings in Arlington County, Va.	5542 N. 11th Rd., Arlington, Va.		Single-Family House	arch. + year unknown		
	13th Rd., intersecting N. Taylor and N. Stuart Sts., Arlington, Va.		Bungalows (scattered Deco-influenced)	arch. + year unknown		
	701 N. Wayne St., Arlington, Va.	Lee Gardens	Garden Apts.	Mihran Mesrobian, arch.		1941–42
	Washington Blvd. + N. Hudson St.	Arlington Main Post office	Public Bldg.	Supervising arch., Treasury Dept.		1937

NOTES

PREFACE

1. Philip Terzian, "Washington Diarist," *The New Republic*, April 23, 1977, p. 44.

2. Gary Wolf, "Transition: The Trans-Lux Theatre Comes Down," letter to the editor, *The Washington Post*, July 4, 1975, p. A-27.

3. James Goode, *Capital Losses: A Cultural History of Washington's Destroyed Buildings* (Washington, D.C., 1979), pp. 378–82, 423–26.

CHAPTER I. THE SPIRIT OF ART DECO

1. See, for example, Ada Louise Huxtable's article "Skyscraper Style" in the *New York Times Magazine*, April 14, 1974, pp. 58–68, and Martin Greif's *Depression Modern* (New York, 1975), pp. 14–16, the latter a particularly strident approach to art history. See also David Gebhard and Harriette Von Breton, *Kem Weber, The Moderne in Southern California, 1920 through 1941* (University of California, Santa Barbara, 1969). David Gebhard, at first partial to the term "Moderne," embraced the use of "Art Deco" in his introduction to *Tulsa Art Deco* (1980).

2. Le Corbusier, *Towards A New Architecture* (1923; London edition, 1948), p. 12.

3. George Howe, quoted in "Modernist and Traditionalist," *Architectural Forum*, July 1930, p. 49.

4. "Can Modern Architecture Be Good?" *The Federal Architect*, October 1930, p. 6.

5. Ralph T. Walker, quoted in *Architectural Forum*, July 1930, op.cit., p. 50. See also Walker's autobiography, *Ralph Walker, Architect* (New York, 1957).

6. Several scholarly works have established the importance of Cret. See Elizabeth Grossman's Ph.D. dissertation, *Paul Philippe Cret: Rationalism and Imagery in American Architecture* (Brown, 1980), Travis McDonald's M.A. thesis, *Modernized Classicism: The Architecture of Paul Philippe Cret in Washington, D.C.* (University of Virginia, 1980), and Theophilus White's *Paul Philippe Cret, Architect and Teacher* (Philadelphia, 1973).

7. Frank Lloyd Wright, *Modern Architecture, Being the Kahn Lectures for 1930* (Princeton, 1931), pp.39–40.

8. Bevis Hillier, *The World of Art Deco* (New York, 1971), p. 23.

9. Roland Stromberg, *European Intellectual History Since 1789* (Englewood Cliffs, N.J., 1975), p. 229.

10. Bevis Hillier, *Art Deco* (London, 1968), pp. 91, 93.

11. Donald J. Bush, *The Streamlined Decade* (New York, 1975), p. 185.

12. Sheldon and Martha Cheney, *Art and the Machine: An Account of Industrial Design in 20th-Century America* (New York, 1936), p. 23.

13. See Jeffrey Meikle's *Twentieth-Century Limited: Industrial Design in America, 1925–1939* (Philadelphia, 1979), passim.

14. Frank Lloyd Wright, *Modern Architecture*, op. cit., p. 35.

15. Sheldon and Martha Cheney, *Art and the Machine*, op. cit., p. 119.

16. Norman Bel Geddes, *Horizons* (Boston, 1932), pp. 288–91.

17. Hillier, *Art Deco*, op. cit., pp. 93–4.

18. Nonetheless, there was architecture of surpassing beauty—preeminently the United States Supreme Court building, completed in 1935—resulting from the classical revival.

CHAPTER 2. WASHINGTON CULTURE IN THE YEARS OF ART DECO

1. Lois Craig and the staff of the Federal Architecture Project, *The Federal Presence: Architecture, Politics, and Symbols in United States Government Buildings* (Cambridge, Mass., 1978), pp. 310–11.

2. Lois Craig, "Hidden Treasures of a Walled City," *A.I.A. Journal*, June 1978, p. 21.

3. Constance McLaughlin Green, *Washington: Capital City*, vol. 2, 1879–1950 (Princeton, 1962), p. 291; and Frederick Gutheim, *Worthy of the Nation* (Washington, D.C., 1977), pp. 174–75.

4. The other members of the board were Milton B. Medary, succeeded after his death by his partner Clarence C. Zantzinger (responsible for the Justice Department building), Louis Ayres (responsible for the Commerce Department building), Arthur Brown, Jr. (Interstate Commerce Commission and Labor Department buildings), William Adams Delano (designer of the circular plaza and the Post Office building—which should not be confused with the old Romanesque Victorian Post Office building nearby), John Russell Pope (designer of the National Archives building), and Louis Simon (Internal Revenue Service building). Bennett was given responsibility for the apex building of the Triangle, which would house the Federal Trade Commission. (Source: Lois Craig, "Hidden Treasures . . ." op.cit., p. 21.)

5. Paul Philippe Cret, "Ten Years of Modernism," *The Federal Architect*, July 1933, pp. 9, 12.

6. "Can Modern Architecture Be Good?" *The Federal Architect*, October 1930, pp. 6, 8–9.

7. William Leuchtenburg, *Franklin D. Roosevelt and the New Deal* (New York, 1963), p. 63.

8. George Peek, with Samuel Crowther, *Why Quit Our Own* (New York, 1936), p. 20.

9. Respectively, the Civilian Conservation Corps, the Works Progress Administration, the Agricultural Adjustment Administration, the Tennessee Valley Authority, and the Public Works Administration.

10. William Leuchtenburg, op.cit., p. 345.

11. Constance McLaughlin Green, op.cit., p. 393.

12. Edwin Rosskam, *Washington: Nerve Center* (New York, 1939), pp. 17, 18.

13. Ibid., pp. 18, 19.

14. More thoroughly classical federal buildings were the Federal Security Agency, the Federal Reserve Board, and Interior Department buildings—and most significantly, the building designed in the Hoover years, but completed in 1935, the Supreme Court. The neoclassical trend continued into the 1940s with the completion of John Russell Pope's designs for the National Gallery of Art and the Jefferson Memorial. Even in the 1950s, the Senate office building later to be named for Everett Dirksen epitomized the trend.

15. Lois Craig et. al., *The Federal Presence*, op.cit., pp. 390–91.

16. Mary E. Van Cleave, "We Pioneers," *Greenbelt Cooperator*, vol. 1, no. 1, (Nov. 24, 1937): 4.

CHAPTER 3. ART DECO — THE ARCHITECTURAL FORMULAS

1. *The Federal Architect*, October 1939, p. 16.

CHAPTER 4. ART DECO COMES TO WASHINGTON

1. Obituary, *Washington Star-News*, June 21, 1974.

2. Obituary, *Washington Star*, July 18, 1972.

3. Obituary, *Washington Post & Times Herald*, January 17, 1958, p. B-2.

4. Obituary, *Washington Post*, September 26, 1975. See also the article by Caroline Mesrobian Hickman, "Mihran Mesrobian (1889–1975): Washington Architect," *Design Action*, May/June 1983, pp. 1–4.

5. John McAndrew, ed., *Guide to Modern Architecture—Northeast States* (New York, 1940), p. 26.

6. The ornamentation was executed by the Edmonds Art Stone Company, a Delaware corporation located in Washington, D.C., and at the time considered the largest plant of its kind in the country.

7. James Goode, *The Outdoor Sculpture of Washington, D.C.* (Washington, D.C., 1974), p. 123

8. Joseph Abel and Fred N. Severud, *Apartment Houses* (New York, 1947), passim.

9. Information supplied by James Goode from an interview with Santmyers's granddaughter.

10. John Perrault, "Report from Miami," *Art in America*, November 1981, p. 52.

11. Glenn Leiner, "Hilyard Robinson and the Langston Terrace Project," unpublished monograph.

12. Even established Art Deco architects like Andre Fouilhoux, who, together with his partner Raymond Hood, had built many famous Art Deco skyscrapers in New York city, earned an award with a pure International Style design.

13. Frederick W. Cron, *The Man Who Made Concrete Beautiful—A Biography of John Joseph Earley* (Fort Collins, Colo., 1977), pp. 5–6.

14. Ibid, p. 4.

15. John Joseph Earley, "Architectural Concrete Makes Prefabricated Houses Possible," *Journal of the American Concrete Institute*, Proceedings, vol. 31, 1935, pp. 513–14.

16. Ibid, pp. 524–25.

17. Typical related buildings were the Southern Railway Building (920 15th Street, NW) and the Potomac Electric Power Company Building (929 E Street, NW), the former completed in 1928 and the latter in 1930. Both were the work of classicist Waddy B. Wood.

18. Cervin Robinson and Rosemarie Haag Bletter, *Skyscraper Style: Art Deco New York* (New York, 1975), p. 12.

19. Wolf Von Eckardt, "Ralph Walker, 'Architect of Century,'" *The Washington Post*, January 19, 1973.

20. Benjamin Forgey, "The Spirit of Silver Spring," *The Washington Post*, Feb. 26, 1983, pp. C-1, C-2.

21. See, for example, the article in *Architectural Forum*, January 1933, on modernization and remodeling.

22. Two Washington buildings received awards: the Hecht Company warehouse at 1401 New York Avenue, NE, and the Hahn's Shoe Store at 1207 F Street, NW.

23. *Architectural Forum*, July 1935, p. 51.

24. Lynne Heneson and Larry Kanter, "Little Taverns: Renovating a Commercial Landmark," *Trans-Lux*, Art Deco Society of Washington, vol. 1, issue 2, February 1983, p. 1.

25. Daniel Vieyra, *"Fill 'Er Up:" An Architectural History of America's Gas Stations* (New York, 1979).

26. Designs were produced by Ely Jacques Kahn, Richard Neutra, R. Buckminster Fuller, Frank Lloyd Wright, William Lescaze, and others. The industrial designer Norman Bel Geddes proposed a service station model to Socony Vacuum Oil Company in 1934, Raymond Loewy submitted a design to Esso in 1934, and Walter Dorwin Teague's design was adopted by Texaco during the late 1930s. One of the earliest design competitions was held by the Union Oil Company of California in 1927.

27. *Architectural Forum*, August 1937.

28. "Hecht's Dedicates New Warehouse," *Washington Star*, Nov. 25, 1936; "Hecht's Company Warehouse One of East's Best," *Washington Herald*, June 30, 1937.

29. For reviews of the Washington Greyhound Terminal in the period's literature, see Manfred Burleigh and Charles F. Adams (eds.) *Modern Bus Terminals and Post Houses* (Ypsilanti, Mich., 1941), p. 141; "Greyhound Terminal of Washington" in *Railroad and Bus Terminal and Station Layout* (American Locker Co., Boston, 1945), p. 89; J. Gordon Carr, "Bus Stations," in Talbot Hamlin (ed.) *Forms and Functions of Twentieth-Century Architecture* (New York, 1952); "Super Terminal," in *Bus Transportation*, April 1940, p. 167; and "New Greyhound Terminal Preview Draws Thousands," *Washington Star*, March 26, 1940.

30. P. Morton Shand, *Modern Theatres and Cinemas* (London, 1930), p. 13.

31. "About Our Title," *Trans-Lux*, vol. 1, issue 1 (November 1982): 1.

32. Michael Kernan, "In Defense of Art Deco," *The Washington Post*, December 6, 1982, p. D-7.

33. When it opened in 1937, Jay Carmody of the *Washington Star* described the building as "a bright thing, modernistic in design and lighting . . . a delight to the eye . . . (and) a sort of H.G. Wells architectural dream come true." (Jay Carmody, "Translux Makes Its Bow At An Unofficial Preview," *Washington Star*, March 12, 1937).

34. For a detailed examination of Eberson's career, see the article devoted to his work in the trade periodical *Theatre Catalog* 7 (1948–49). Included is a full-length photographic view of the Silver Theater and its adjoining shopping center.

35. A Baltimore theater by Zink—also named the "Senator"—remains in almost perfect condition.

36. Ray Burkett and Randee Bernstein, "Deco 'Echoes' in Former Washington Amusement Park," *Trans-Lux*, vol. 1, issue 2 (February 1983): 6–8.

37. Frederick W. Cron, *The Man Who Made Concrete Beautiful*, op. cit., pp. 49–51.

38. "Annex to the Congressional Library," *The Federal Architect*, October 1939, pp. 15–17.

39. Paul Philippe Cret, "Ten Years of Modernism," *The Federal Architect*, July 1933, p. 8.

BIBLIOGRAPHY

BOOKS AND DISSERTATIONS

Abel, Joseph H., and Severud, Fred N. *Apartment Houses*. New York: Reinhold Publishing Corp., 1947.

American Locker Company. *Railroad and Bus Terminal and Station Layout*. Boston, 1945.

Appelbaum, Stanley. *The New York World's Fair 1939/40*. New York: Dover Publications, 1977.

Applewhite, E.J. *Washington Itself: An Informal Guide to the Capital of the United States*. New York: Alfred A. Knopf, 1981.

Arwas, Victor. *Art Deco*. New York: Harry N. Abrams, 1980.

Arwas, Victor. *Art Deco Sculpture*. New York: St. Martin's Press, 1975.

Balfour, Alan. *Rockefeller Center: Architecture as Theatre*. New York: McGraw-Hill, 1978.

Bel Geddes, Norman. *Horizons*. Boston: Little, Brown & Company, 1932.

Burleigh, Manfred, and Adams, Charles M. *Modern Bus Terminals and Post Houses*. Ypsilanti, Mich.: University Lithoprinters, 1941.

Bush, Donald J. *The Streamlined Decade*. New York: George Braziller, 1975.

Cerwinske, Laura. *Tropical Deco: The Architecture and Design of Old Miami Beach*. New York: Rizzoli International Publications, 1981.

Cheney, Sheldon, and Cheney, Martha. *Art and the Machine: An Account of Industrial Design in 20th-Century America*. New York: Whittlesey House, 1936.

Cox, Warren J., Jacobsen, Hugh Newell, et al. *A Guide to the Architecture of Washington, D.C.* New York: McGraw-Hill, 1974.

Craig, Lois, and the staff of the Federal Architecture Project. *The Federal Presence: Architecture, Politics, and Symbols in United States Government Buildings*. Cambridge, Mass.: M.I.T. Press, 1978.

Cron, Frederick W. *The Man Who Made Concrete Beautiful: A Biography of John Joseph Earley*. Ft. Collins, Colo.: Centennial Publications, 1977.

Gebhard, David, and Von Breton, Harriette. *Kem Weber: The Moderne in Southern California, 1920 through 1941*. Santa Barbara: University of California, 1969.

Gebhard, David, and Von Breton, Harriette. *L.A. in the Thirties, 1931–1941*. Layton, Utah: Peregrine Smith, Inc., 1975.

Goldberger, Paul. *The Skyscraper*, New York: Alfred A. Knopf, 1981.

Goode, James M. *Capital Losses: A Cultural History of Washington's Destroyed Buildings*. Washington, D.C.: Smithsonian Institution Press, 1979.

————. *The Outdoor Sculpture of Washington, D.C.* Washington, D.C.: Smithsonian Institution Press, 1974.

Green, Constance McLaughlin. *Washington: Capital City, 1879–1950*. Princeton, N.J.: Princeton University Press, 1962.

Greif, Martin. *Depression Modern: The Thirties Style in America*. New York: Universe Books, 1977.

Grossman, Elizabeth. *Paul Philippe Cret: Rationalism and Imagery in American Architecture*. Ph.D. dissertation, Brown University, 1980.

Gurney, George. *Sculpture and the Federal Triangle*. Washington, D.C.: Smithsonian Institutioon Press, 1984.

Gutheim, Frederick. *Worthy of the Nation: The History of Planning for the National Capital*. Washington, D.C.: Smithsonian Institution Press, 1977.

Gutman, Richard J.S., and Kaufman, Elliott. *American Diner*. New York: Harper & Row, 1979.

Henneke, Susan P., ed., Gebhard, David, Johnson, Carol N., et al. *Tulsa Art Deco: An Architectural Era, 1925–1942*. Tulsa, Okla: Junior League of Tulsa, 1980.

Hillier, Bevis. *Art Deco*. London: Dutton Studio Vista, 1968.

———. *The World of Art Deco*. New York: E.P. Dutton & Co., 1971.

Hirshorn, Paul, and Izenour, Steven. *White Towers*. Cambridge, Mass.: M.I.T. Press, 1979.

James, Theodore, Jr. *The Empire State Building*. New York: Harper & Row, 1975.

Justement, Louis. *New Cities for Old*. New York and London: McGraw-Hill, 1946.

Karp, Walter. *The Center: A History and Guide to Rockefeller Center*. New York: American Heritage Publishing Company, 1982.

Kreisman, Lawrence, and Gardaya, Victor. *Art Deco Seattle*. Seattle, Wash.: Allied Arts of Seattle, 1979.

Leich, Jean Ferriss. *Architectural Visions: The Drawings of Hugh Ferrris*. New York: Whitney Library of Design, Watson-Guptill Publications, 1980.

Lescaze, William. *On Being an Architect*. New York: G.P. Putnam's Sons, 1942.

MacKertich, Tony, and MacKertich, Peter. *Facade: A Decade of British and American Commercial Architecture*. New York: Stonehill Publishing Co., 1976.

McDonald, Travis. *Modernized Classicism: The Architecture of Paul Philippe Cret in Washington, D.C.* M.A. thesis, University of Virginia, 1980.

Meikle, Jeffrey. *Twentieth-Century Limited: Industrial Design in America, 1925–1939*. Philadelphia: Temple University Press, 1979.

Mesrobian, Caroline Isabelle. *A Selection of the Architectural Oeuvre of Mihran Mesrobian, Beaux-Arts Architect, Washington, D.C.* M.A. thesis, Tulane University, 1978.

Morrison, Andrew Craig. *Theatres of Washington*. Washington, D.C.: Theatre Historical Society, 1972.

Myer, Donald Beekman. *Bridges and the City of Washington*. Washington, D.C.: U.S. Commission of Fine Arts, 1974.

Naylor, David. *America's Picture Palaces*. New York: Van Nostrand Reinhold, 1981.

Pildas, Ave. *Art Deco Los Angeles*. New York: Harper & Row, 1977.

Pildas, Ave. *Movie Palaces*. New York: Clarkson Potter, 1980.

Protoppapas, John, and Brown, Lin, eds. *Washington on Foot*. Washington, D.C.: Smithsonian Institution Press, 1984.

Robinson, Cervin, and Bletter, Rosemarie Haag. *Skyscraper Style: Art Deco New York*. New York: Oxford University Press, 1975.

Rosskan, Edwin. *Washington: Nerve Center*. New York: Alliance Book Corporation, 1939.

Stern, Rudi. *Let There Be Neon*. New York: Harry N. Abrams, 1979.

Stone, Susannah Harris. *The Oakland Paramount*. Berkeley, Calif.: Lancaster-Miller Publishers, 1981.

Sullivan, Donald C., and Danforth, Brian J. *Bronx Art Deco Architecture*. New York: Hunter College, City University of New York, Publishing Center for Cultural Resources, 1976.

Teague, Walter Dorwin. *Design This Day*. London: The Studio Publications, 1946.

Varian, Elayne H. *American Art Deco Architecture*. New York: Finch College Museum of Art, 1974.

Vieyra, Daniel K. *"Fill 'er Up": An Architectural History of America's Gas Stations*. New York: Collier Macmillan Publishers, 1979.

Vlack, Don. *Art Deco Architecture in New York, 1920–1940*. New York: Harper & Row, 1974.

Walters, Thomas. *Art Deco*. New York: St. Martin's Press, 1973.

Weinstein, Iris, and Brown, Robert K. *Art Deco Internationale*. New York: Quick Fox, 1977.

White, Theophilus. *Paul Philippe Cret, Architect and Teacher*. Cranbury, N.J.: Associated University Presses, 1973.

Works Progress Administration, Federal Writers' Project. *Washington: City and Capital*. Washington, D.C.: Government Printing Office, 1937.

Wright, Frank Lloyd. *Modern Architecture, Being the Kahn Lectures for 1930*. Princeton, N.J.: Princeton University Press, 1931.

PERIODICALS, GENERAL

Architecture (AIA Journal), American Institute of Architects, December 1983.

The American Architect, International Publications, Inc., New York.

Architectural Forum, Rogers and Manson Corp., New York.

Architectural Record, F.W. Dodge Corp., New York.

The Federal Architect, Association of Federal Architects, Washington, D.C.

Pencil Points, Pencil Points Press, Inc., New York.

Trans-Lux, Art Deco Society of Washington, Washington, D.C.

PERIODICALS, BY AUTHOR

Hickman, Caroline Mesrobian. "Mihran Mesrobian (1889–1975): Washington Architect." *Design Action* 2, no. 3 (May/June, 1983).

Huxtable, Ada Louise. "Skyscraper Style." *The New York Times Magazine*, April 14, 1974.

Sawtelle, Mark C. "Diner." *Historic Preservation*, Sept./Oct., 1979.

NEWSPAPER ARTICLES, BY AUTHOR

Carlin, Barbara. "Greenbelt Architectural Find: Center School Styled in Pure Art Deco." *Prince George's Post*, Feb. 3, 1983, p. 5.

Chamblee, Andrea. "Compromise to Save Art Deco School." *Prince George's Post*, Aug. 18, 1983, p. 1.

Forgey, Benjamin. "Defying the Times: Old Sparkle Restored at the Little Taverns." *The Washington Post*, Dec. 24, 1983, p. C-1.

————. "Rerouting the Bus Station: The Flight to Unveil the Romance of Art Deco," *The Washington Post*, March 31, 1984, pp. G-1 and G-3.

Hirshfeld, Max, and Allan, Henry. "D.C.'s Deco." *The Washington Post Magazine*, April 16, 1978.

Kernan, Michael. "The Age of Art Deco." *The Washington Post*, Sept. 3, 1982, p. C-7.

Kernan, Michael. "In Defense of Art Deco." *The Washington Post*, Dec. 6, 1982, p. D-7.

Oman, Anne H. "Deco Echoes." *The Washington Post*, Weekend Section, March 20, 1981.

Rathbun, Elizabeth. "A Protest for Art's Sake: Fight is on to Save Facade in Greenbelt." *Prince George's Journal*, Aug. 2, 1983, p. A-1.

Timberlake, Joan. "Washington's Art Deco has a Style of Its Own." *The Washington Times*, magazine section, March 24, 1983, p. 4-D.

Timmermans, Germaine. "Art Deco Devotees Appalled at Proposed Plans for Replacement of Center School." *Greenbelt News-Review*, July 28, 1983, p. 1.

Wynter, Leon. "Rallying 'Round a Symbol of Greenbelt." *The Washington Post*, Aug. 17, 1983, p. C-1.

ARCHIVAL SOURCES

American Institute of Architects Library

Columbia Historical Society

District of Columbia Buildings Permits, Microfilm Reading Room, National Archives and Records Service

Horydczak Collection, Prints and Photographs Division, Library of Congress

Washingtoniana Room, Martin Luther King Library, District of Columbia Public Libraries

INDEX

128